THE LITTLE BOOK OF

Restorative Teaching Tools

Published titles include:

The Little Books of Justice & Peacebuilding present, in highly accessible form, key concepts and practices from the fields of restorative justice, conflict transformation, and peacebuilding. Written by leaders in these fields, they are designed for practitioners, students, and anyone interested in justice, peace, and conflict resolution.

The Little Books of Justice & Peacebuilding series is a cooperative effort between the Center for Justice and Peacebuilding of Eastern Mennonite University and publisher Good Books.

THE LITTLE BOOK OF

Restorative Teaching Tools

Games, Activities, and Simulations for Understanding Restorative Justice Practices

LINDSEY POINTER, KATHLEEN MCGOEY, AND HALEY FARRAR

New York, New York

Good Books books may be purchased in bulk at special discounts for sales promotion, corporate gifts, fund-raising, or educational purposes. Special editions can also be created to specifications. For details, contact the Special Sales Department, Good Books, 307 West 36th Street, 11th Floor, New York, NY 10018 or info@skyhorsepublishing.com.

Good Books is an imprint of Skyhorse Publishing, Inc.®, a Delaware corporation.

Visit our website at www.goodbooks.com

10 9 8 7 6

Library of Congress Cataloging-in-Publication Data
Names: Pointer, Lindsey, author. | McGoey, Kathleen, author. | Farrar, Haley, author.
Title: The little book of restorative teaching tools : games, activities, and simulations for understanding restorative justice practices / Lindsey Pointer, Kathleen McGoey and Haley Farrar.
Description: New York, New York : Good Books, [2020] | Series: The little books of justice & peacebuilding | Includes bibliographical references.
Identifiers: LCCN 2019049285 (print) | LCCN 2019049286 (ebook) | ISBN 9781680995886 (trade paperback) | ISBN 9781680995893 (epub)
Subjects: LCSH: Critical pedagogy. | Restorative justice. | Youth with social disabilities--Education. | Activity programs in education--Social aspects. | Educational games.
Classification: LCC LC196 .P64 2020 (print) | LCC LC196 (ebook) | DDC 370.11/5--dc23
LC record available at https://lccn.loc.gov/2019049285
LC ebook record available at https://lccn.loc.gov/2019049286

Series editor: Barbara Toews
Cover design: Mona Lin
Cover photograph: Howard Zehr
Chapter 8 illustrations: Colleen McGuire

Paperback ISBN: 978-1-68099-588-6
eBook ISBN: 978-1-68099-589-3

Printed in China

Table of Contents

1.
Introduction

Have you ever sat down in a class or training, excited to engage in a discussion about important issues, only to experience a long lecture with PowerPoint slides, ending in an unstructured invitation for "Questions?" or "Thoughts?" Have you noticed that it is the same few voices that always chime in, while the rest of the class is silent?

Have you ever been part of a class or training where the teacher begins a conversation on a controversial topic without first taking the time to build the relationships, trust, and structure for that conversation to be respectful? Have you noticed feelings of exclusion, shame, misunderstanding, or intimidation in yourself and others?

Have you ever spent a day in a class or training participating in engaging activities, building trust and relationships with other participants, and left feeling happy and connected, only to realize that the group never talked about any important or meaningful topics? Have you wished that you could have engaged in an open conversation about issues that really matter with that supportive group?

Most of us have experienced all three of these learning scenarios at one time or another. Sometimes relationship and trust building are missing, and as a result, the class lacks the sense of safety necessary for a productive conversation to occur. Sometimes a well-structured and intentional framework to dialogue about important issues is missing, and the group loses the opportunity to learn from each other's experiences and perspectives. Sometimes both of these important factors are missing. Even within the restorative justice community, where cultivating relationships, respectful communication, and ensuring equal voice are central goals, teaching spaces still often fall into one of these traps and fail to deliver the connected, courageous, honest, and empowering learning experiences we need.

The use of games and activities as teaching tools offers an antidote to this problem. Games are interactive and fun and naturally build relationships in a group, creating a strong foundation of trust and comfort that makes respectful conversations about challenging issues possible. The shared experience of a game presents a clear structure and entry to begin important dialogue that allows participants to learn from each other. Students leave the class feeling engaged, informed, and energized, as does the teacher. Our hope is that this book will encourage you to experiment with this style of teaching and provide helpful insights and example games to get you started. Be prepared for an increase in laughter, fun, and deeper, more impactful learning experiences.

Why Bring This Style of Teaching to Restorative Justice Practices?

Social institutions often serve to reinforce existing power structures, elevating the voices of those who are already heard and further marginalizing those who are not. The conventional criminal justice system provides a pertinent example of this phenomenon. Within the court space, the voices, perspectives, and opinions of the judge and lawyers are elevated (both by the physical structure and the procedure of the court process) above the voices of both the responsible party and the harmed party. While diversity in the legal field is slowly improving, typically this means the voice of an affluent, white, male legal professional is given greater time, attention, and importance than the voices of the participants in the process, who are frequently racial minorities with less economic opportunity. This contributes to pervasive racism in the criminal justice system, which routinely disadvantages people of color.

The restorative justice movement has, in many ways, been able to disrupt this hierarchy by providing a social space, in the form of the circle or conference process, in which the voice, story, and perspective of each participant is valued equally. While this impact does not always extend beyond the culmination of the restorative justice process, it can serve as a liberatory experience for those present, in which relationships of power and oppression are recognized and countered. More needs to be done, however, as restorative justice in its current form is often criticized for failing to challenge these systems of domination and for privileging the voices of some over others. David Dyck, in particular, has noted that the restorative justice

3

field has been largely dominated by white, middle- to upper-class professionals who have focused too much on individual responsibility and interpersonal facilitation skills. This has resulted in an ignorance and dismissal of the influence of broader contextual factors and the way that societal structures benefit some at the expense of others and ultimately fuel crime.[1] Fania Davis argues that in order for restorative justice to be successful, we must endeavor to repair not just interpersonal harm, but also the sociohistorical conditions and institutions that perpetuate harm.[2] For example, a school falls short if it only implements restorative justice as a response to individual cases of student misconduct and fails to apply restorative principles to transforming the policies, practices, and individual biases that consistently advantage white students and disadvantage students of color. Restorative endeavors in schools must address zero-tolerance policies, the high rates of suspension and expulsion of African American students compared to their white classmates, and the criminalization of student behavior through the presence of police officers in schools.

From a restorative justice perspective, the perpetuation of social inequities ought to be viewed as a large-scale harm in dire need of reparation. Particularly because structural inequity so often precipitates crime, it is the responsibility of restorative justice practitioners to expand our focus to address these broader social conditions and to uphold restorative values while working within or alongside other social institutions.

Educational spaces, from formal academic classrooms to community trainings, are similarly guilty of creating systems of domination and elevating the voices of those who already hold power over those who do not. In educational contexts, the teacher or trainer is often presented as the only one holding and imparting valuable information in the classroom. This power arrangement inevitably sustains and reinforces inequitable power structures in broader society. When the teacher's voice is heard and valued above all others, preexisting hierarchies are reinforced and marginalized students are further silenced. The capacity of education to contribute to greater structural and social transformation is thus hindered.

The spaces and organizations in which we teach and train others in restorative justice are a ripe place to begin the transformation towards a more just and equitable society. Education has long been lauded for its capacity to spark social transformation when it is done in a way that is empowering and enlivening to learners, especially those who have typically been excluded from other segments of society. Davis explains that from slavery times to the present, "black people have treasured education as liberatory."[3] She further notes,

> Author and educator bell hooks continued this black tradition, exhorting educators to enact a revolutionary pedagogy of resistance that is profoundly anticolonial and anti-racist. This is education as the practice of freedom, as famed critical pedagogist Paulo Freire puts it, and it means implementing practices that both challenge curricular and pedagogical biases that reinforce systems of domination like racism and sexism while simultaneously creating innovative ways to teach diverse groups of students.[4]

Teaching on restorative justice with a pedagogy grounded in restorative values may also be liberatory and lead to greater social transformation. When the voices, stories, and perspectives of each student are valued and heard equally alongside the teacher, the systems of power and privilege that impact every aspect of our social lives can be revealed. The students and teacher become more conscious of their beliefs and biases, as well as their individual and collective roles in those systems. Games and activities create the opportunity, structure, and trust that support the equal voice necessary for this to take place.

A group of teachers learning restorative justice practices through games and activities have the opportunity to reflect on the varying experiences, backgrounds, and needs of their students and on their own experiences as teachers and students. They learn from self-reflection (What was empowering and what was destructive about my school experience? What are the privileges or disadvantages I've had as a result of my identity?) and hearing others' reflections. Systemic harms that may have previously seemed distant, abstract, or insurmountable come into focus when exemplified through specific individual experiences. Teachers begin to understand how institutionalized oppression and implicit bias cause and perpetuate harm. Participants emerge with a sense of responsibility to discuss these insights and work for social justice in their schools and beyond.

It is the aim of this book to explore methods for teaching restorative concepts and skills in alignment with restorative values. Toward this end, this book offers games and activities as effective tools for creating a highly participatory learning environment that engages the voices, perspectives, and experiences of all present. As authors, we recognize that we have primarily lived on the benefiting side of society's harmful power structures. Each author identifies as a white, cisgender, heterosexual woman of US American nationality. The majority of our experiences working in the restorative justice field have taken place in Longmont, Colorado, and Wellington, New Zealand, two relatively affluent, predominantly white communities. It is therefore especially important that we recognize and take responsibility for our own role in perpetuating the forces of imperialist, white supremacist, capitalist patriarchy at play in the United States and elsewhere and consciously endeavor to counter it. In order to confront our privilege and the ways it may be implicitly or explicitly exercised in the classroom, we have committed to evaluation of course delivery and outcomes through observation, self-reflection, and sincere consideration of learners' feedback and critique. Throughout this book, there is frequent mention of the self-awareness, growth, and constant learning necessary in order to teach in this way. This is an ongoing process for each of us.

A Note on Language
The material in this book is intended to be applicable across learning contexts, including restorative practices trainings and academic classrooms (within

universities, schools, or elsewhere). For reasons of simplicity and clarity, we have chosen to primarily refer to the person most responsible for facilitating an experience as the *teacher* or *instructor* and those participating in the experience as *learners* or *students*. However, when teaching in this way, that relationship is not nearly so binary. The teacher is also always a student, and the student is likewise also a teacher. We refer to the learning environment as a *class* or *training*.

Chapter Overviews

This book is divided into two parts. Chapters 2–4 establish the theoretical basis for using games and activities to teach restorative justice practices. Chapters 5–7 contain practical guidance on how to create a restorative learning experience, prepare yourself to facilitate the experience, and design your own games. The final chapter offers a variety of games to get you started. Each chapter begins with a short story that captures an experience of the authors and their colleagues utilizing restorative teaching tools. The stories touch on one or more of the games outlined in Chapter 8 and illustrate an important theme of that chapter.

Chapter 2 provides an introduction to restorative pedagogy, a paradigm of teaching in alignment with restorative values and principles. It makes the case for the use of games and experiential activities as a central restorative teaching strategy. From there, it further examines how teaching in a restorative way redistributes power and contributes to greater racial and social justice in the learning community by giving voice to those who have typically been marginalized in the classroom.

Chapter 3 draws on relevant literature from the field of experiential learning and discusses how its principles align with the restorative ethos through equally valuing the voice, perspectives, and experiences of all present and encouraging students to apply the learning to their lives.

Chapter 4 provides an overview of the concept of a restorative community, a social organization in which all activities, systems, and communication are in alignment with restorative values. It discusses how restorative learning communities can be built and strengthened through the use of games and activities.

Chapter 5 offers more holistic guidance on how to facilitate a restorative learning experience. Undertaking the recommendations put forth in this book with fidelity to restorative values asks that you reflect deeply on who your learners are, who you are, and how you will maintain awareness of the complex dynamics of the learning process. This chapter provides guidelines for how to maintain this commitment as you implement the activities described in Chapter 8.

Chapter 6 describes how to design games and experiential activities for teaching restorative practices, including how to write scenarios and lead an effective debrief of a game or activity to deepen learning. This chapter is intended to spark your own creativity in designing pedagogical activities that will fit the needs of your learning community.

Chapter 7 explains how to design an activity-based learning experience. Building on the conceptual frameworks outlined in Chapters 2–4 and the step-by-step instructions for creating your own activity described in Chapter 6, Chapter 7 offers guidance on how you can assemble the "full package" of your training or class, including preparation, design, delivery, and self-reflection.

Chapter 8 provides in-depth instructions for facilitating pedagogical games and activities and for debriefing the experience with participants. The games and activities are organized by different topics and skills that a restorative educator may wish to teach. The games and activities included in this book have been tried and tested in a range of learning contexts (including community-based practitioner trainings and academic classrooms) with learners of different ages. While they are primarily intended for use with high school students, university students, and adults, they may be adapted for younger learners as well.

2.
Restorative Pedagogy[1]

While playing "Out of the Box" with a group of high school students, a student joked that his team should just google the answer. "You never said we couldn't google it!" he shouted. We laughed as a group about what results we might get from googling "How can Jordan who likes to draw cartoons and make silly videos repair the harm from stealing Alex's-skateboard," referencing the scenario we were using for the activity. After the joking and laughter died down, I asked, "What if we google 'Colorado penalties for misdemeanor theft'?" The group agreed that Google would have a clear answer for that search. Next, I asked, "So if Google can give us answers for the conventional criminal justice system so easily, why isn't Google helpful in restorative justice?" This started a fruitful conversation that surfaced some of the main points that differentiate restorative justice from the conventional justice system. The students talked about how restorative justice considers the circumstances of the individuals involved and takes into account the specific harms they have experienced. It is the collective brainpower of the people in the circle considering the individuals involved, their strengths, and the harms experienced that allows those factors to be synthesized into creative ideas to repair harm.

—Lindsey Pointer

This story speaks to why restorative practices need to be taught differently than other disciplines. Whereas in other disciplines, there may be one correct answer to a question, in a restorative approach, there will inevitably be many varied "correct" responses. This is because the individuals involved and their distinct experiences always inform the outcome. We must find ways of teaching that allow us to practice understanding the complicated worlds of individuals, the social structures and institutions that influence our lives, and the ways in which we are all connected. As restorative practices and the teaching of restorative practices spread around the world, scholars, practitioners, and educators have begun to ask these very important questions: How should restorative practices be taught? What teaching structures and methods are appropriate in forming a restorative pedagogy?

This chapter serves as an introduction to restorative pedagogy, a paradigm of teaching in alignment with restorative values and principles. It makes the case for the use of games and experiential activities as a central restorative teaching strategy. It further examines how teaching in a restorative way redistributes power and contributes to greater structural transformation through giving voice to those who have typically been marginalized in the classroom. In this way, experiential learning can function as a liberatory pedagogical practice, just as the restorative justice process can function as a liberatory practice for participants.

Teaching in Alignment with Restorative Values and Principles

In the traditional paradigm of teaching, often referred to as the "Transmission Model," the teacher transfers knowledge to the students, generally through lectures.[2] The instructor is normally situated at the front of the classroom, delivering knowledge to a group of students who take notes. Paulo Freire has referred to this method of teaching as the "banking" concept of education, "in which the scope of action allowed to the students extends only as far as receiving, filing and storing the deposits made by the teacher."[3] The teacher has absolute control as the authority figure, determining course content, objectives, and outcomes. This encourages a passive approach to learning on the part of students.

From the viewpoint of a restorative framework, there are a few problems with this education model. Whereas restorative approaches prioritize equal voice and emphasize the facilitation of a space where all voices are valued, the traditional classroom values and creates space for the teacher's voice above all others, establishing a clear hierarchy. Additionally, the traditional classroom structure encourages a passive role for students, a conformist approach to learning, and sometimes an adversarial sense of competition resulting from the grading structure of the course.

All of these qualities contradict the participatory, individualized, and collaborative nature of restorative processes. It is interesting to note that this approach to teaching shares many similarities with the dominant criminal justice system, in which a punishment is assigned to a passive offender within a court ritual marked by hierarchy and adversarial interactions.

Because of this contradiction, traditional instructor-centered teaching strategies are particularly unsuitable for restorative practices courses, regardless of context. Restorative practices classrooms or training spaces should instead seek to build and engage community, while modeling the values and principles central to the restorative justice process. As Belinda Hopkins notes, "The restorative mindset inevitably impacts on pedagogy. A restorative teacher who works with her students ensures that how she teaches simultaneously models her own restorative values but also develops restorative values, aptitudes and skills in her students."[4]

So how might restorative pedagogy align with the restorative values and worldview? The restorative worldview sees humans as fundamentally relational beings, intricately connected to one another and to their environment.[5] The values that emerge from this worldview include respect, accountability, participation, self-determination, nonviolence, humility, trust, and transformation. It is the mission of the restorative justice movement to transform individuals and social structures to be in alignment with this worldview and the core restorative values. This includes influencing the way in which restorative practices are taught. Restorative educators must ask themselves: What learning structure will communicate and reinforce the restorative values? How can we better value the perspectives of the students in the room in addition to the teacher's? How can education encourage the development of empathy?

Critical and Feminist Pedagogies: Education as a Liberatory Practice

The emerging restorative pedagogy is in alignment with a new paradigm of teaching that has been gaining popularity in recent decades, in which students and teachers jointly construct knowledge, share power, and learn cooperatively in the classroom while promoting the development of relationships. The origin of this new paradigm is found, in part, in the writings of Paulo Freire and the development of critical pedagogy. Freire advocates for "liberating education," which helps students to recognize and confront domination and take action to end oppression.[6] In critical pedagogy, students and teachers engage in meaningful dialogue to learn from each other, ultimately promoting a more democratic and egalitarian society.

Dialogue between the students and teacher is a central component of critical pedagogy, which helps to challenge the hierarchy inherent in traditional teaching methods and to empower all parties in the learning process. As Freire explains, "Through dialogue, the teacher-of-the-students and students-of-the-teacher cease to exist and a new term emerges: teacher-student with student-teachers."[7] Student and teacher are jointly responsible for participating in the learning process and continually growing through it.

Feminist pedagogy, a contemporary expression of critical pedagogy, broadens the focus to more

15

intentionally include gender, race, sexuality, age, and nationality. bell hooks is an advocate for critical and feminist pedagogy who emphasizes the importance of building community in the classroom through taking time to really get to know students. In hooks's classroom, everyone is recognized and valued as individuals, and as she explains, "This insistence cannot be simply stated. It has to be demonstrated through pedagogical practices."[8] In this way, the classroom becomes a democratic setting in which everyone feels a responsibility to contribute. Each student is an active participant, not a passive consumer. This engenders a respect for multiculturalism, because the value of each individual voice and experience is recognized.

This active engagement with vulnerability must pertain to the teacher as well. The teacher must be willing to share, grow, and be fully present alongside the students. This may prove difficult for some teachers because they fear losing control. However, it is necessary in order to create the desired climate of openness, trust, and shared risk-taking. Teachers who use circle practice with students are already experienced in releasing control and power in order to fully participate and trust in the process, though this is often the biggest challenge.

"As a classroom community, our capacity to generate excitement is deeply affected by our interest in one another, in hearing one another's voices, in recognizing one another's presence."
—bell hooks, on creating an enjoyable learning experience

These insights from critical and feminist pedagogy align with restorative values and provide ample inspiration for the further development of restorative pedagogy. Through flattening the hierarchy of the classroom and giving voice to the thoughts and experiences of those who are often marginalized, the act of learning can contribute to greater structural transformation. When students' voices are elevated, students and teachers learn from each other's perspectives and build a shared understanding of structural issues along with a motivation to bring about change. Games and activities provide an effective vehicle for creating this equalizing, engaging, and dialogue-promoting learning environment.

Restorative Justice Education as a Liberatory Practice

Teaching restorative practices in a way that is grounded in the insights of critical and feminist pedagogies has the potential to expand the transformative impact of restorative justice. A prominent critique of restorative justice is that in its focus on making amends at an interpersonal level, it fails to address larger, structural injustices. As Dyck explains,

> One of the most persistent critiques of the field of restorative justice as it is manifested in the practical activities of community programs around the world is that it still fundamentally fails to address structural dimensions of criminal conflict. Its critics argue that current restorative programming focuses too much energy on the interpersonal dimensions of crime and ignores the deeper roots of the trouble as found

in class, race/ethnicity, and gender-based systemic conflict.[9]

This shortcoming is due in part to the fact that practitioners are generally not trained to think about restorative justice work within a systemic, structural frame of reference and therefore, by default, tend to focus solely on personal responsibility without understanding the structural roots of the conflict or wrongdoing. In order to remedy this, practitioners need to be trained not only in interpersonal communication skills, but also in the ability to recognize and address the way in which the actions of those who the public may perceive as "problem people" actually reflect larger systemic problems.

Dorothy Vaandering has similarly argued that common theoretical frameworks used in the restorative justice field such as Reintegrative Shaming Theory and the Social Discipline Window maintain a harmful focus on the "victim" and "offender" and what "occurs within their individual psyches while failing to take account of the institutional and structural forces at play in shaping the beliefs and actions of individuals."[10] The contributing context in which the harm occurred is often ignored. Vaandering asserts that critical theory ought to inform and strengthen restorative justice practice, allowing the process to move beyond a narrow focus on individual behavior. When these systemic, institutional, and structural dimensions are considered, the restorative justice conference itself can function as a liberatory practice for participants.

Just as a restorative justice conference that adequately considers the structural roots of an incident can function as a liberatory practice, so can learning about restorative justice through a mode of teaching grounded in restorative values. Barb Toews notes that restorative justice education can produce similar outcomes to a facilitated process, including the opportunity to speak about personal experiences, personal change and growth, and a desire to engage in positive relationships and give back to the community. As Toews explains,

> This pedagogy, based on restorative values, aims to inspire individual and social transformation; build community among participants; give voice to the unique experiences of participants; offer opportunities for real-life problem solving; provide a creative learning environment that is co-created by students and facilitators; view students as practitioners, theorists, and educators; and invite instructors to view themselves as students and share in the learning process.[11]

In order for these greater transformative outcomes to be achieved, the learning process needs to create space for students to speak to their individual experiences and perspectives as they relate to course material and for those contributions to be honored by the group. Together, students and teacher grapple with what they have shared with each other and consider the meaning for their lives and for the world. This represents a crucial shift from an attempt to teach about social and structural issues in the abstract to a classroom that actively challenges these issues through building a shared lived understanding and a motivation to address the roots of crime and conflict.

3.
Experiential Learning and Restorative Justice

The game "Shovel Face" gives students the opportunity to practice the facilitation skill of asking follow-up questions on the spot and builds empathy for how it feels to be the responsible or harmed party in a restorative justice process. Students experience the vulnerability of being asked to talk about a major life experience in a circle of people and gain a first-hand understanding of what is required to feel safe, respected, and heard in that space.

Once, while playing "Shovel Face" with a group of adults, a participant responded to the initial question of "What has been the greatest learning experience of your life and what did you learn?" with a story about breaking the law as a teenager. The follow-up questions her classmate asked prompted her to reflect on the factors in her life that contributed to the behavior. She described her school and family experiences and shared about being arrested and her defiant response to the punitive sanctions she received. In the debrief following the activity, she explained how telling her story during the game gave her a better perspective on how difficult participating in restorative justice is for responsible parties, how much the process asks of them, and how that understanding would influence her as a facilitator. Other participants dialogued about how hearing her reflections helped them better understand some of the factors that lead to crime and why punishment often makes things worse.

The learning from this game was deep because it emerged organically from an authentic experience. Rather than being told that participating in restorative justice is a difficult and vulnerable experience for responsible parties and that a person's life circumstances contribute to the decision to commit a crime, the participants had the opportunity to experience that learning together, while practicing an important facilitation skill.

—*Lindsey Pointer*

A key characteristic of restorative pedagogy is an experiential mode of teaching. It is important that students not only learn about restorative practices, values, and principles, but also experience them directly. The field of experiential learning is well-developed and offers a wealth of insight for the enhancement of restorative pedagogy. The principles of experiential learning include equally valuing the voices, perspectives, and experiences of all present and encouraging students to apply the learning to their lives. Many of the central values and principles of experiential learning are in clear alignment with restorative ideals, making the integration of experiential approaches into the teaching of restorative practices a clear choice. This experience of working together, valuing each other, and learning from each other can translate into big-picture changes outside the classroom.

An Introduction to Experiential Learning

Experiential learning is learning through doing. As John Luckner and Reldan Nadler describe, "It is a process through which individuals construct knowledge, acquire skills, and enhance values from direct experience."[1] Facilitated experiential learning generally involves a few distinct phases. Students engage in an activity, reflect on the activity, derive useful insights from that analysis, and then incorporate the new learning into their understanding and behavior. Games and activities provide a highly effective mode of experiential learning that can be less intimidating to learners than other more direct experiential teaching methods such as role-plays.

The benefits of experiential learning are numerous. Increasing the involvement of learners leads to an increase in interest and ownership of what is being learned. It also encourages students to take responsibility for their own learning and behavior, rather than assigning that responsibility to a teacher or other outside person. This way of learning also encourages a more complete integration of what has been learned with the learner's perception of self, thoughts, and actions moving forward.

23

In experiential exercises such as games, the role of the teacher more closely resembles the role of a facilitator who creates a space for the experience and helps to facilitate a meaningful, reflective discussion following the activity.[2] The instructor is no longer the "expert" imparting her knowledge to students. She is instead a facilitator who participates in the learning experience. This allows for a more even distribution of power and voice between teacher and students, bringing the classroom further into alignment with restorative values.

In her role as facilitator, the instructor is responsible for creating and maintaining a respectful space for the learning activity. She structures the experience of the game, sets boundaries, and supports learners. Learning takes place largely through a debrief of the game or activity that supports reflection, analysis, and synthesis. The debrief also allows the instructor to assess the needs of the students and make appropriate modifications to subsequent games and activities.

As an experiential learning method, games and activities rely on the wisdom of the group to make learning happen, just as restorative processes rely on the wisdom of the circle. Learners are involved in posing questions, being curious, being creative, drawing connections, and constructing meaning. They are co-creators of the learning experience. The instructor sets up an activity and holds the space for the learners' engagement but is not in control of the exact outcome. That is up to the students.

One of the challenges in experiential learning is knowing how far to push participants out of their comfort zone. It can be difficult to know what game

"Learning cannot focus only on individuals; it must also direct attention to the relationships between and among the people involved. The experiences, needs, and perspectives of all learners, including educators, matter and are central, not in contrast to or in competition with one another, but in relation to one another."
—Kristina Llewellyn and Jennifer Llewellyn, on a restorative approach to learning[3]

or activity will present the right level of challenge for the group. The teacher must be intentional and pick experiences that are right at the edge of unfamiliar territory for a group's comfort level. There will be feelings of discomfort or risk. At this edge space, learners can go for it and have an experience of success or a breakthrough. Finding this "edge" by reading the group and maintaining an appropriate level of challenge throughout a class or training is yet another skill that must be carefully honed by those teaching restorative practices.

A supremely important characteristic of learning experientially is that it is fun. Playfulness and laughter create an invitation for active involvement, building a sense of togetherness and community that aids the learning process and aligns with restorative values. Through incorporating fun, energy is high, attention is focused, and the drive to learn is enhanced through sheer enjoyment of the process.

In part because of this high level of engagement and involvement, experiential learning creates a highly relational classroom environment. Relationship-building helps to establish trust between students and cultivate a more connected learning community. This focus on relationships is fundamental to restorative approaches. Games contribute to creating a fun, safe, and relaxed atmosphere, which aids in relationship building.

Examples of Experiential Learning in Restorative Practices Classrooms

Experiential teaching methods have already been implemented in a range of restorative justice learning contexts with great success. This commitment to integrating experiential learning activities grounded in restorative values and priorities has been made in schools, university classrooms, and restorative justice education programs in prisons, among others.

There are a few experiential and relational exercises that are commonly used to teach in a way that aligns with restorative values, the most common of which is the circle. An entire lesson may be structured with the circle framework, giving students the opportunity to reflect on their learning in the circle and providing the teacher with valuable feedback about the students' current needs. The circle also prevents dominant students from monopolizing the conversation and ensures equal opportunity to speak and listen.

Pair and group work is also often used to encourage open dialogue between learners. This can serve to build relationships within the class and provide space for learners to share their own experiences with the material and how it applies to their lives. This group work often includes opportunities to apply material to case studies in order to gain a real-life understanding of restorative justice. This may be done through role-plays of the restorative justice process. Some restorative justice classes have even given students real facilitation roles in their communities, providing students with the experience of effecting positive change through a community restorative justice process, followed by the opportunity to reflect on the real-life impact of the process in the classroom.[4]

Students are also often encouraged to engage in self-reflection and implementation within their own communities. Barbara Carson and Darrol Bussler report asking students to identify and examine their own values as they relate to justice, design new means for implementing restorative approaches in troubled areas, and practice restorative processes in their communities.[5] Kristi Holsinger notes that one outcome of the restorative justice course she delivered to a combined group of traditional college students and incarcerated youth was that students learned how to apply the principles of restorative justice to their personal lives and discovered new ways to deal with the conflicts and problems they face.[6] Students' development of self-awareness enhances the liberating potential of education by allowing them to understand their own reactions, biases, and contexts.

Games are often used in restorative justice educational spaces as a way to break the ice and build relationships and trust prior to beginning a lesson or circle process. While they are certainly effective ice-breakers, their use as a restorative teaching method need not end there. Games may also be used as an experiential learning exercise to deepen students' understanding of restorative justice and develop specific skills related to facilitating and participating in restorative processes. The element of play enhances the experiential aspect of the learning environment by encouraging students to take risks and learn from mistakes while also building community.

4.
Building a
Restorative Learning
Community

A restorative justice class or training that includes lots of games and activities that build relationships and encourage meaningful conversations builds a powerful sense of community within the group. Students often talk about feeling like they "found their people." They frequently seek out further opportunities to be together and want to invite others to be part of the community.

One example of this community-building phenomenon occurred at Victoria University of Wellington. At the beginning of the year, all residential advisors (RAs) working in the dorms are trained in restorative practices. The training is highly interactive, composed almost entirely of games and activities. During the second year of implementation, a group of RAs decided that they wanted to establish a

*Restorative Justice Club. They met regularly to prac-
tice facilitating circles and to continue improving
their skills and understanding of restorative justice
through additional games and activities. They also
endeavored to spread the knowledge and understanding of restorative approaches on campus and
recruited new club members. The formation of this
club speaks to the strong experience of community
that emerges through restorative learning.*

—Lindsey Pointer

This chapter provides an overview of the restorative
community concept, a social organization in which
all activities, systems, and communication are in
alignment with restorative values. It discusses how
restorative learning communities can be built and
strengthened through the use of games and activities.

Games and activities create a social space in which
learners can experience voice, participation, and transformation, often resulting in similar outcomes to the
restorative justice process itself. In a restorative learning community, students' perspectives are honored and
respected, and they are encouraged to consider the
applicability of the learning to their lives and the world.

Building Restorative Communities

The restorative practices field has experienced
immense growth in recent decades. What began
as an effort towards criminal justice reform has
since expanded into a social movement dedicated
to making restorative practices integral to everyday
life and moving families, schools, communities, and
society towards more peaceable ways of interacting.
As Christopher Marshall explains, this restorative

social movement has the broad aim of the "creation of interpersonal relationships and societal institutions that foster human dignity, equality, freedom, mutual respect, democratic engagement and collaborative governance."[1]

The vision of a restorative community involves the regular and widespread use of restorative practices that build relationships, provide a sense of fairness and justice, and facilitate healing. It also involves going about basic community functions in a way that nurtures "just relations," or relationships characterized by mutual respect, care, and dignity,[2] and honors our innate connection to one another. In describing the philosophical grounding of restorative practices, Howard Zehr makes a connection between the beliefs and practices of restorative justice and the concept of *shalom*.[3] Shalom is often translated as "peace," but actually implies a broader vision that emphasizes "right" or "just" relationships between individuals, between groups, between people and the earth, and between people and the divine. It emphasizes the connectedness of all things and provides a helpful philosophical basis for the expansion of restorative practices into other areas of social life. Davis draws on the southern African concept of *ubuntu* in her description of the restorative ethos.[4] Ubuntu means "a person is a person through their relationships" and speaks to humans' connection to each other, as well as to the natural world. Restorative communities are those which embrace and encourage this awareness of our interconnectedness.

The inspiration for this expansion of the restorative justice vision lies largely in the work of schools, which were the first communities to extend the range of restorative practices beyond disciplinary measures to include relationship-building and intentional efforts to change school culture. This innovation fostered a new understanding of restorative work as involving both the restoring and the proactive building of positive relationships. Through this development, restorative schools have provided a model for how other organizations can function in a more relational and restorative way. Universities, workplaces, churches, community groups, prisons, and even entire cities have since endeavored to follow in this mission of becoming restorative communities.

Restorative Learning Communities

So how can "just relations" and an awareness of our interconnectedness be fostered and reinforced proactively in the classroom or other learning environments?

Kristina Llewellyn and Christina Parker identify four different classroom environments and approaches to teaching characterized by different combinations of controlled or close relationships and minimizing or maximizing "conflict dialogue." They find that classrooms with controlled relationships, in which the teacher relies on lecture-based, top-down delivery of information with little space for student voice, encourage passive learning and provide little opportunity to share divergent or varying perspectives. The absence of relationality in these learning communities enables the continued privilege of normative identities because the identities of those most marginalized are excluded. This ultimately maintains the power dynamics of the status quo and prevents the sparking of greater societal change. In contrast to a controlled learning environment, a restorative approach to education prioritizes close relationships. The value of each individual voice and background in the classroom must be recognized, thus engendering respect for the wide range of experiences and perspectives in the learning community.

According to Llewellyn and Parker, the restorative learning community will also seek to maximize conflict dialogue, which they define as dialogue that fosters "critical reflection on social and conflictual issues."[5] This requires confrontation of social systems of oppression and the facilitation of more inclusive relationships. When teachers maximize conflict dialogue in close relationships, they increase opportunities for greater inclusion of marginalized and diverse students and their histories, experiences, and perspectives. This has a positive impact on student learning, societal inclusion, and civic engagement.

As restorative practitioners and educators, the authors have each observed the impact of cultivating close relationships and encouraging conflict dialogue in the learning space. Through the highly relational environment of the restorative learning community, learners realize that their own stories have meaning and weight in informing the wisdom of the group. They become motivated to discern and distill their own beliefs and values. The participatory approach elicits these beliefs, values, and ideals, and sparks dialogue within the group. As learners feel ready to explore and discuss their own worldviews, they discover connection or disconnection with beliefs held by others. This resonance or dissonance, when facilitated through conflict dialogue that respects all voices, sets the stage for deeper examination of social issues.

Frequently, the learner's first participation in a restorative learning space provides validation that they are not alone; there are others who are similarly motivated by a hope that individuals truly have the capacity to effect change. As the learning process continues, however, the learner will likely experience discomfort as their previously held beliefs (often built upon judgment and assumptions) are dismantled or challenged. The whole group may find itself accessing the fertile space where new ways of understanding and perceiving may emerge.

bell hooks highlights the crucial role that a trusting community plays in providing such a space within diverse educational settings. In an interview with her friend and colleague Ron Scapp, hooks inquires, "What has most changed about your thinking in the last ten years as you have attempted to create greater awareness of the need for non-biased ways of knowing?" Scapp replies,

> The single most important realization has been the need to establish a genuine sense of community based on trust . . . and not just expertise and knowledge . . . [Educators] working with diverse populations are challenged to recognize the importance of genuine commitment to the well-being and success of all students and not simply those deemed worthy because they come from privileged backgrounds.[6]

In a trusting community, learners are willing to share more vulnerably and courageously, even when that means going beyond commonalities and moving into the risky territory of identifying differences. It is this honest discussion of differences that can give rise to discovery of previously unforeseen options for transforming conflict. As hooks explains, "Lots of people fear encountering difference because they think that honestly naming it will lead to conflict. The truth is our denial of the reality of difference has created ongoing conflict for everyone."[7]

Supported by the trust that emerges through intentional facilitation and relationship-building, students feel more courageous to name their own personal hardships, hopes, and the systemic forces limiting those hopes. Observations or perspectives that may be deemed controversial or offensive may be shared and processed in a group committed to courageous vulnerability and respect. By prioritizing a highly relational, non-hierarchical group dynamic, facilitators can encourage the conflict dialogue that allows learners to take bigger risks in identifying their own role in empowering—and oppressing—the voices and freedoms of others and the resulting personal and collective responsibility derived from that awareness. While the cultivation of this awareness is important for all participants, it is particularly crucial to encourage such realizations in individuals from privileged backgrounds.

Games and activities are especially well suited to cultivating a learning community that is highly relational and provides a platform for conflict dialogue about complex social issues to take place. They produce dialogue that honors the perspectives of all present and reinforce an inclusive community concept. Games contribute to creating a fun, safe, and relaxed atmosphere, which aids in relationship building and fosters trusting spaces for challenging conversations to take place. Beyond the conducive atmosphere they generate, games may also contribute to relationship building on a deeper level, in the same way that the restorative justice process itself impacts relationships between participants.

Restorative Rituals and Games

Restorative justice is well-regarded for the positive impact it has on relationships, often shifting participants towards a more connected and caring way of being together through the course of the process. What exactly causes this positive shift in emotions and relationships is a relatively new area of inquiry and several scholars, including Meredith Rossner, John Braithwaite, Jane Bolitho, and Vernon Kelly, have offered insightful theories.

One possible explanation for the transformative impact of restorative justice lies in Victor Turner's theory of ritual. Through bringing participants into a distinct social space, apart from normal social life, characterized by equality and respect, the restorative justice process brings participants into a "liminal space."[8] According to Turner, in this liminal space, normal social rules, roles, and hierarchies are suspended, and "communitas"—or, the revelation that all people are connected in one equal, undifferentiated community—may emerge.[9] Through this revelation, participants experience a greater sense of interconnectedness, empathy, and an impulse towards kindness.

Ritual theory tells us that wherever they are found, liminal spaces facilitate connection and strengthen relationships. Games, like rituals, have also been noted for their ability to foster liminality, through providing a social space where participants can step outside of normal social rules and roles, experiencing greater equality and connection.[10] Through generating liminal spaces, games facilitate interaction between people across social boundaries, including race, ethnicity, gender, nationality, socio-economics, political parties, and more.[11]

Games provide a strong social lubricant and can even help transform animosity to amity.

In theories of play, this liminal space is often called the "magic circle."[12] Within the magic circle, participants may experience a profound engagement, equality, and connection akin to the communitas Turner describes in ritual experiences.[13] This leads to enhanced feelings of trust and belonging. The magic circle of the game also creates a feeling of safety. Within the game, participants are free to take risks and try something new without worry of judgment or negative repercussions. This trust and safety contribute to the effectiveness of games as a learning modality.

Games and activities help to create and sustain a highly relational classroom environment by cultivating an awareness of our innate connection that fosters empathy and kindness. Through providing a feeling of safety and a chance to step away from the normal rules, roles, and restrictions of daily life, games and activities offer a social space in which individuals' differing perspectives and challenging community issues can be discussed in a way that equally values the voices of all. By facilitating highly relational interactions, stimulating conflict dialogue, and cultivating liminal spaces, games and experiential activities help to build a restorative learning community that reinforces and deepens restorative values.

5.
Preparing to Teach

While facilitating "Build the Nest" with a group of adult learners in a restorative practices course, a fruitful conversation was sparked by a mock case scenario involving a physical fight between two male Latinx students and two male Caucasian students at their high school. As we moved into the Sub-System and System levels of conflict, participants began sharing more personal points of view. A Latinx member of the group chose to voice his own experience in the Sub-System Conflict realm. He explained that in elementary school, a teacher repeatedly called him and another Latinx student "trouble-makers" in front of the class and regularly sent them to detention for the same behaviors white students exhibited without consequence. He explained that it felt like she expected him to misbehave just because of his race and didn't make an effort to actually get to know him. The hurt, confusion, and anger of being labeled based on his teacher's assumptions around his racial and cultural identity still lingered years later.

I watched and listened as this participant's sharing led the group into a courageous discussion about their own experiences related to structural violence and bias. The conversation was possible because the game had elicited the personal experiences of participants. The scenario and exercise opened up a brave space for this student to want to voice his painful experience and for it to become a learning opportunity for everyone, including me.

—Kathleen McGoey

This chapter offers holistic guidance on how to facilitate a restorative learning experience. Facilitating a learning experience that welcomes risk, elicits challenging discussion, and supports transformation requires great responsibility. Undertaking the recommendations put forth in this book with fidelity to restorative values asks that you reflect deeply on who you are, who your learners are, and how you will maintain awareness of the complex dynamics of the learning process.

As a teacher of restorative practices, you must go beyond thinking about *what* you are teaching and deeply reflect on *how* you teach and *how* you relate to learners. When leading a group of learners to the edge of their comfort zone in an effort to facilitate new perspectives and understanding, be prepared to participate authentically in the experience of transformation yourself by practicing vulnerability and transparency. You will often find yourself at the edge of your comfort zone as well! This chapter sheds light on your responsibility to be conscious of your choices and their impacts, and how to integrate the essential values of love, humility, humor, and empathy in creating an environment that invites everyone present to learn and grow.

The Need to Know Yourself

The need for the teacher to engage in an ongoing process of self-reflection cannot be overstated. Teachers of restorative practices must constantly think about how to see beyond specific topics to the relational components affecting learning and reflect critically on what they are bringing to the learning community. Ask yourself, how are you sharing power with learners? How are you checking your own biases and assumptions? How are you contributing to a cooperative learning experience that creates a brave space for you and learners to engage in conflict dialogue? When those conversations are uncomfortable for you, what tools do you use to stay present and non-reactive? Realize that at times, you may feel stuck by fear, doubt, and failure. Be prepared for trial and error.

Teachers must reflect on their own role in the web of connectivity that ties them to students and others. Because violent patterns exist in relationships, it is also within relationships that one finds the ability to transcend violence. Where might you be perpetuating patterns of violence or dominance yourself, however inadvertently? Where might values like exclusion, revenge, or retribution appear in your thoughts and actions? Acknowledge your own non-binary existence as someone who has at times been harmed and also caused harm to others. How do your own experiences (with family, education, the criminal justice system, community, etc.) affect how you relate to teaching restoratively?

41

Authenticity and Congruence

In order to bring your full, real, honest self to the web of relationships in the learning setting, strive for congruence. Carl Rogers names congruence as a necessary condition in effective patient-therapist relationships,[1] and it is also essential in the teaching context. Congruence in the restorative learning community means that teachers, like learners, choose to represent themselves accurately through deep awareness of self. Teachers must confront their own biases courageously and revise their own beliefs based on their emerging learning with students. Acknowledging your own doubts, lack of experience, and challenges increases a sense of mutual respect, raises the bar for learners, and ultimately creates a richer experience for you as well.

It is impossible to be in a state of congruence at all times, but committing to a mindfulness practice or other method aimed at increasing self-awareness will make a difference. While teaching, often this mindfulness appears in the moment in the form of a pause that allows you to observe before reacting. In that pause, you may reflect on what might be upsetting about the present moment. The pause is a form of respect that creates space for compassion. Within the pause, you may also realize the need to let go, to loosen the reigns of control as participants direct their own experience. Or, you may recognize that you have moved outside your own window of tolerance and need to employ a self-regulation method and return to a place where you can be most effective. Consider being transparent with learners when you utilize a pause or other approach for bringing self-awareness to the present. Such modeling is invaluable in demonstrating congruence because it allows learners to see what is real for you in the moment.

Meditative practices are often thought of as the most effective way to cultivate mindfulness, but they are not the only option. Some choose to increase self-awareness through writing, dance, music, exercise, self-talk, or a therapeutic modality. The next section offers a summary of two useful tools you can apply immediately to guide processes of self-evaluation and reflection. Develop an ongoing practice that helps you come into greater congruence with your authentic self. This congruence should carry with it feelings of clarity, centeredness, serenity, and trust. Ongoing critical self-reflection is a requirement of teaching restorative practices, so if one method doesn't work for you, continue exploring.

Two Tools for Mindfulness, Self-Evaluation, and Self-Reflection

The following tools are complementary and may be used before, during, and after teaching a class or training. The first provides a step-by-step strategy for self-observation of intent and action while teaching, with the goal of integrating a respectful and restorative approach. The second outlines questions to clearly establish a teacher's identity, teaching statement, and evaluation process in relationship to a particular topic or class. The value and impact of these tools increase when they are implemented with consistency and transparency.

P.A.²I.R.: A Guide for a Mindful Restorative Approach

In her article guiding educators to utilize mindfulness-based restorative practices, Annie O'Shaughnessy emphasizes the importance of taking a mindful pause. She notes that this pause helps a teacher or facilitator bring more awareness and an open mind and heart to their learners. The mindful pause interrupts reactions based on patterned judgments or assumptions and, instead, cultivates compassionate curiosity, from which a more empathetic and restorative response may arise. O'Shaughnessy provides the acronym P.A.²I.R. to prompt this mindful approach:

- **Pause:** As you approach the behavior, take a deep, even breath—in through your nose and out through your mouth. Intentionally drop assumptions you hold. Allow at least three seconds to pass.
- **Assess:** Bring awareness to your own experience. For example, "Am I escalated?" Check your understanding of what you know to be observably true. Notice your intention as you approach (Barron and Grimm, 2006). For example, do you simply want to make the student feel bad?
- **Acknowledge:** Begin the interaction with the student by acknowledging what you notice, what is observable and true. "I am noticing . . ." "It seems . . ." "I see that . . ."
- **Inquire:** Ask restorative questions to learn more, to intentionally dismantle your assumptions and encourage self-reflection. "What's happening for you?" "What need were you trying to meet?" (Remember, if they are escalated they might not be able to really know.)

- **Restore/Repair:** Collaborate with the student to come up with ways to restore themselves to the class or in relationship with you, or simply to self-regulate.[2]

O'Shaughnessy points out that it is necessary for the facilitator to recognize if either they or the student do not have the capacity for a meaningful restorative dialogue in the moment and to delay the conversation until all participants have self-regulated.

Identity Memos, Teaching Statements, and Self/Course Evaluations

Toews writes that restorative justice pedagogy asks an instructor to engage in critical reflection of themselves, their course material, and their teaching strategies. She describes identity memos, teaching statements, and self/course evaluations as three tools that help guide the reflection and evaluation process.[3] These tools are particularly effective when used together, as the identity memo and teaching statement help establish standards for evaluating the course and one's own teaching.

Applied in a teaching context, the identity memo sheds light on assumptions, biases, and experiences that a teacher brings to their role and how those things influence the class, the learners, class evaluation, and outcomes. Toews advises sharing the memo with others for feedback to surface biases and assumptions that were not previously identified. She gives the following prompts to help formulate an identity memo prior to teaching a restorative justice course:

1. Personal and professional experiences with victimization and offending.

2. Experiences and perspectives on privilege, power, racism, poverty, and structural injustice.
3. How those experiences and perspectives:
   a. Relate to your interest in restorative justice
   b. Inform your understanding of what restorative justice is and is not, its goals, and promise and pitfalls.
4. Ability to actively listen to and respect the experiences and perspectives of others and transform your own thinking.
5. Assumptions about victims, incarcerated individuals, each of their respective advocates or service providers, and correctional staff and administration.[4]

In a teaching statement, the teacher identifies their motivations, beliefs, goals, and strategies related to the specific topic and context of their teaching. The teaching statement may be shared with learners to stimulate dialogue that will clarify expectations and improve the teaching approach according to learners' needs. In this way, the teaching statement gives students a voice in the design and delivery of the learning experience. Toews offers these questions to outline a teaching statement:

1. What is motivating you to teach restorative justice?
2. What is your goal for the educational effort(s)?
3. What values support your teaching efforts and to what degree do those values resonate with restorative justice and/or transformative education?

4. What teaching practice will you do or have you done to achieve your stated goals using your values set?
5. How will you give life to the values of restorative justice pedagogy?[5]

We, the authors, would add to this list:

6. What are the unique needs of my learners, and how will I create a dynamic learning environment that is responsive to those needs?
7. How will I create brave spaces so that all voices are heard?
8. What tools will I use to self-regulate in the moment when I am challenged and uncomfortable as a facilitator?
9. How will I remain present and support a culture of playfulness and resilience?

Toews provides a third table with questions to guide course and self-evaluation. The evaluative process is circular and ongoing, beginning at the point of course preparation, continuing throughout the duration of the course, and informing subsequent course material and teaching methods. To be done effectively, the evaluation is collaborative and incorporates feedback from the teacher, learners, and others involved in class design and delivery.

1. To what degree did your teaching practices:
   a. Promote or hinder student expression of personal experiences and perspectives?

    b. Connect to the real-world experiences of the students?

    c. Communicate respect for students?

    d. Engage students in collaborative problem-solving?

    e. Uncover new understandings of restorative justice and its practices?

    f. Create opportunities for the students to be the teachers?

2. How did the class influence you in terms of:

    a. Challenging your assumptions about crime and justice?

    b. Raising awareness about your experiences with power, privilege, racism, and other forms of structural and institutional violence?

    c. Expanding or modifying your understanding of restorative justice and its promise and problems?[6]

Cultivating Empathy

To create an environment where learners can participate courageously and authentically, be prepared to hold space for their raw emotions and perceptions. A teacher hoping to facilitate a transformative learning experience needs to help others feel heard, loved, and accepted. Just as a facilitator in a restorative justice process understands that a person must not be defined by one decision or behavior, a restorative practices teacher does not demonstrate an approving or disapproving attitude based on what a learner thinks or says. Instead, practice relating to learners with empathy, characterized by a genuine willingness to accept the learner wholly, without condition. When a learner is given full permission to express their perspective truthfully, an empathetic teacher can both validate what is shared and offer reflection that introduces new meaning that will deepen a learner's understanding of self.

It is the teacher's responsibility to create a foundation of trust that invites the discomfort and risk-taking necessary for honest and authentic participation by students and teachers alike. Prepare to integrate and uphold the guiding norms of the "brave space" in order to invite courageous contributions from both learners and teachers. The "brave space" is distinguished from the "safe space" in that it acknowledges that a learning process that involves the letting go of formerly held perspectives to make way for new understanding and transformation inherently demands discomfort and risk. Instead of proposing a learning experience that is free from harm or difficulty, the brave space emphasizes the need for courage through five basic ground rules: (1) explore controversy with civility, (2) own your intentions and your impact, (3) challenge by choice, (4) respect self and others, and (5) no attacks or violence, which requires a clarifying conversation to distinguish the difference between a personal attack and challenging an individual's statement or belief.[7] Actively engage with these norms before, during, and after the class.

"We strongly encourage facilitators who use the brave space framework to strive for protracted dialogue in defining brave space and setting ground rules, treating this conversation not as a prelude to learning about social justice but as a valuable part of such learning. We have found that so doing allows us as facilitators to demonstrate openness to learning from participants, thereby disrupting and decentering dominant narratives in which knowledge flows one way from teachers to students."
—Brian Arao and Kristi Clemens,
The Art of Effective Facilitation [8]

Consider how you relate to the norms and how learners from dominant and marginalized communities will have differing needs for courageous participation to take place. These norms can become a compass for managing brave spaces that empower the voices of students during difficult conversations about individual and systemic issues.

Keep in mind that you never know fully what is happening, or has happened, in the lives of others. In moments of frustration or exasperation, mindfulness can play a role in regaining perspective and replacing judgment with curiosity. Expect to encounter some learners who seem completely shut off and do not ignore them. Demonstrate the same unconditional attitude of welcome and engagement, and trust that they will eventually respond, even if you don't see change immediately. Remember that a student may also shut off because of something you have done or said. Reflect on the scenario and allow it to drive inquiry and growth. Make it clear through your words and actions how students can speak up if they have an issue with something you are doing. Be proactive and check in with a student if something seems wrong.

Once, while facilitating a circle during a restorative justice training in a men's prison in New Zealand, I used a talking piece that was a gift from the 2017 National Association of Community and Restorative Justice conference in Oakland, California. The talking piece has a Black Power fist on it, a tie to the tradition of racial justice activism in the Oakland community. I had brought the talking piece as a symbol of how restorative justice has grown into a social movement, but hadn't considered the impact it would have in the community I was entering. I introduced the talking piece and asked the first circle question, passing the piece to the man on my left. He looked down at it and immediately burst out laughing, holding it up for the rest of the circle to see. What I had not considered was that Black Power is one of the major gangs in New Zealand, and the group I was working with was mostly members of the Mongrel Mob, a rival gang. Thankfully, the relationships and trust were built up enough in our group that they were able to laugh and make fun of me and I could learn from my mistake. I share this embarrassing story as an illustration of how important it is to create a space where students can speak up when they have an issue with something you have said or done. Often it will result in a conversation that everyone can learn from.

—Lindsey Pointer

When you choose to implement these recommendations, teaching will be both fulfilling and demanding. Practice empathy with yourself. Respect students by listening to their needs and feedback; respect yourself by being patient as you face your own mistakes, biases, and judgments. Seek to be an eternal learner. If at any point you find yourself becoming passive in your relationship with learners or with the material, take a break, ask for help, and replenish. Reach out to people who are not part of your learning community and ask for their perspective. They may be able to provide fresh insight and bolster your confidence when you are feeling depleted. The authors engage in this self-exploration on an ongoing basis. By working in collaborative communities, they access energy and resources to work with joy, love, and hope, while holding each other accountable in this profound process of transformation.

The Need to Know Your Learners

Pay careful attention to who your learners are, and where the class and activities might take them. How will you practice seeing and treating students as individuals and encourage them to actively voice their opinions and stories? On the other hand, how will you know when students have been pushed beyond their comfort zone and are unable to participate constructively in the moment? How will you reestablish safety and trust in the class if this occurs?

Because restorative pedagogy values a high level of engagement and participation by learners, teachers must be conscious of the inner conflicts that students may be confronting, especially those related to class, race, gender, ethnicity, legal status, and other aspects of identity. hooks' experience addressing race with university students provides a clear example of why a teacher's level of awareness is so important. In her efforts to bring students into honest communication about race and anti-racism, hooks noticed that when their inner conflicts were not acknowledged, students were likely to hold on even more tightly to what was familiar, and refused to engage with difficult conversations about diversity, to the extent that they sometimes shut down altogether.[9]

Learning restorative practices often catalyzes a process of change in fundamental beliefs and behaviors. To be done well, restorative practices are implemented holistically, driven by a restorative mindset at the individual and community level, which requires a significant paradigm shift. Educators who are hoping to elicit this shift must find ways of operating that are more about *being* restorative than *doing* restorative. This asks the teacher to approach learners and their lives with patience, compassion, empathy, and curiosity.

Risks and Choice

Pay attention as you guide your group of learners towards the edge of their comfort zones, using the same skills you use as a restorative justice facilitator to track the needs of each individual and the group as a whole. Managing that delicate space, watching for signs of fear and insecurity, and continuing to make activities challenging, but not too challenging, are the artful tasks asked of teachers in a restorative learning environment. Learners are asked to let go of their preexisting concrete notions in order to engage in meaningful inquiry that allows for complexity.

This is the ripe place from which a group of learners may go deep and step fully into the brave spaces that transform perspectives. This process requires openness and critical thinking, which reinforces self-determination and the recognition in learners that they are responsible for their futures.

Choosing to step into the unknown is crucial if learners are to candidly address structures of dominance and make more conscious choices to change such structures. Support them in developing their capacity to speak and listen with respect, to state clearly their own thoughts and beliefs, even when this may spark difficult conversation. Returning to the example of discussing race and confronting racism, hooks notes the need to close the gap between theory and practice. She observes that while most US citizens are opposed to overt acts of racist terror or violence and state they wish to see an end to racial discrimination, it has been easier to engage with written critiques of racism than it has been to find constructive ways to talk about it, and from there develop constructive actions.[10] A fear of conflict or concern they will say the wrong thing is often at the heart of people's resistance to sharing their perspectives. Frequently, it is the most privileged individuals (including the teacher) who struggle most with owning and speaking about racial biases. When working with white students on unlearning racism, hooks prioritizes the value of embodying risk to help students come to terms with the fact that circumstances in which conflict is present are not actually negative and should be approached with tools to cope with conflict instead of avoiding it and distancing ourselves from those circumstances.[11]

Creating consciousness around racism leads to the realization that racism is not innate; it is always about choice. The first step then is for people to become aware of their own beliefs and assumptions that consciously or unconsciously perpetuate violence through racism and other forms of discrimination. Ideally, through that awareness, there emerges the responsibility of choice and the understanding that every person has the opportunity to decolonize their minds and change their beliefs and assumptions, which in turn changes thoughts and behavior. This process of discovery and choice is just as critical for a teacher as it is for a student.

The Art of Facilitating Risk-Taking

As a teacher facilitating learning experiences that involve risk-taking, you will need to be prepared to respond to a range of reactions from learners. While it is appropriate for learners to feel some degree of challenge and discomfort within the brave space that is essential for transformation and change, it is also necessary to note when you or your learners may be moving outside the zone where optimal learning can occur. Daniel Siegel's "window of tolerance" provides a helpful tool with signs that can indicate if your learners have moved outside of this optimal learning zone into a hyperarousal state (fight or flight), which involves feeling emotionally reactive, defensive, inse-cure, or enraged. In the other direction, you may note signs of hypoarousal (immobilization) in learners, which involves feelings of absence, inability to think, shame, passivity, numbness, or shutting down.[12]

Ideally, when people are operating within their window of tolerance, they are feeling safe, curious, open, empathetic, and holding a clear sense of their own and others' boundaries. Moving people beyond this window by forcing them to participate in activities, not taking time to build trust and relationship, or allowing conversations to devolve into shaming-blaming sessions is detrimental to the individual growth experience and damaging to the trust you seek to build in your learning community. Consider how the dynamic of your and your students' identities may affect their ability to take risks. Intentionally assembling a teaching team that reflects the diversity of your students is integral in making risk-taking safer for students. Know that you will make mistakes and do your best to stay conscious and curious about what comes up for you and learners as you take on risk and conflict dialogue. Refer to restorative values and draw on restorative processes when trust is lost or damaged.

Love, Humor, and Humility: Values to Help with Hard Conversations

While it is important to reverently hold space for the discomfort and intensity of difficult conversations about topics like race, it also falls on the teacher to find ways to help learners feel a sense of joy in learning, so that they can feel they have enough internal resources to return to those hard conversations. Integrating humor, love, and humility will help establish a foundation of trust so that your community of learners will be willing to take risks and choose to move towards productive conflict dialogue.

"When as teachers we teach with love, combining care, commitment, knowledge, responsibility, respect, and trust we are often able to enter the classroom and go straight to the heart of the matter."

—bell hooks, *Teaching Community*[13]

Bringing this understanding of love into the learning setting supports learners in thinking about their opinions and critically examining the beliefs and perceptions informing those opinions.

Humor is essential in helping both teachers and learners laugh at themselves and avoid a defeating sense of hatred for self and others when discovering uncomfortable truths. This may be particularly relevant for learners from privileged groups as they uncover feelings of despair or self-hatred brought about by knowledge of the impacts of their heritage. Humor should not minimize the gravity of the revelation, but instead encourage a sense of faith and hope that this knowledge is the seed of change. Humility helps us remember that everyone is imperfect, and in that imperfection, each person has the opportunity to derive meaning from their experiences, uncertainties, and processes of change. Keep the spirit of love, humility, and humor alive as you design new activities and prepare the learning experience.

6.

How to Design an Experiential Activity for Teaching Restorative Practices

As I coach new volunteers through their first several experiences facilitating community restorative justice processes, the most common feedback I offer is to use more reflective statements and to practice reframing inflammatory or unhelpful statements. My coworkers and I agree that reflecting and reframing are two of the most essential skills needed by facilitators to take on more high-stakes cases and effectively manage the "difficultator" (our term of endearment for that person most likely to throw a curveball severe enough that it could make the whole restorative justice process go sideways).

Reflection and reframing require a facilitator to think on their feet, sometimes in a moment when they may feel uncomfortable, uncertain, or escalated. Knowing we could use an experiential activity to address this need, we created "Mirror Mirror" and "Race to Reframe." These games provide a low-pressure way to practice these important skills. While "Mirror Mirror" can be used early during a class to generate connection while practicing reflective statements, "Race to Reframe" works well at the end of a class because it adds an element of time pressure and gets people laughing and competing. After several deliveries of "Race to Reframe," we recognized it was necessary to increase the offensiveness of the statements needing to be reframed, in order to push the skill development of our advanced facilitators. We continue to revisit and adapt both games according to the context and skill level of the group in order to keep them fun and challenging.
—Kathleen McGoey

This chapter describes six steps for designing games and experiential activities for teaching restorative practices, including how to write scenarios and lead an effective debrief of the game or activity to deepen learning. These aspects of design and delivery are intended to help learners to understand the connection between the "micro" learning experience and the larger "macro" issues, concepts, or skills being taught.

Designing an Activity Step 1: Cultivate Self-Reflection and Willingness to Learn
The first step in the process of designing a restorative experiential learning activity is taking the time

to reflect on your own relationship to and understanding of a topic. This will include identifying and considering your relevant history, assumptions, and biases. In order to be an effective teacher, you must be willing to learn through the teaching process.

A question for educators: "Am I willing to transform in the process of helping my students transform?"

—Edward Taylor, *Transformative Learning Theory*[1]

Before you begin the design process, take the time to sit with your own needs and assumptions related to the topic or discuss them with other practitioners. How does this learning activity relate to your own worldview and notions of a desired future reality?

This process of self-reflection is ongoing. A sincere examination of one's frames of reference is likely to lead to feelings of unsettledness, doubt, and vulnerability. Be ready to experience discomfort and significant personal shifts as you participate in this process, and consider who you may reach out to in order to discuss and understand this discomfort.

Designing an Activity Step 2: Identify a Need and Establish a Learning Objective

Next, identify a need in your learning community that you would like to address through the activity. Is there a certain skill or concept that your learners are struggling to grasp? What issue would you like to explore with the group? For example, maybe you work with a group of facilitators who are struggling to generate open-ended questions during the facilitation process and need to practice that skill. Or perhaps you have noticed your learners are not grasping the potential for creativity in responding to individual harms in the agreement-making phase of the restorative justice process. A group of new learners may need an activity that will help them understand what differentiates the restorative approach to crime and conflict from more conventional approaches. On a conceptual level, you may have noticed that your learners are too focused on the interpersonal dynamics of cases and are not grasping how larger structural inequities contribute to crime and conflict. Being aware of and responsive to your learners' needs in this way will help you to present the right level of challenge for the group to facilitate transformative learning.

Once you have identified a specific need for learning in your community, establish a related learning objective or aim. For example, for the needs identified in the previous paragraph, the learning objective of your activity may be:

- Learners will practice the skill of generating open-ended questions on the spot.
- Learners will explore the purpose and potential of the agreement-making phase of the restorative process.
- Learners will experience what differentiates restorative approaches from other approaches.
- Learners will understand and engage critically with the larger structural roots of crime and conflict.

Once you have a clear learning objective established, you will be able to return to that objective throughout the design and debrief process to make sure you are achieving your aim.

Designing an Activity Step 3: Get Creative, Employ Models and Metaphors

Once your learning objective is clearly established, it is time to engage your creativity. What will help your learners grasp the new skill or concept? Is there a conceptual model or a metaphor that would help participants "get it"? How could you use that metaphor or conceptual model creatively in designing your activity? Learning often takes place through the imaginative use of metaphors or an engaged and interactive use of visual models.

Many of the games and activities included in Chapter 8 revolve around metaphors or conceptual models. For example, a game designed to help students explore how to respond to specific harms and draw on individual strengths in the agreement-making phase employs the metaphor of thinking "outside the box" as a way to highlight the importance of creative thinking. The game is titled "Out of the Box," and participants literally free themselves from a physical box through generating creative agreement ideas as a team. A game called the "Social Discipline Window Shuffle" encourages learners to engage deeply with the conceptual model of the Social Discipline Window by asking them to step into a giant version of the model and act out or describe the different approaches in relation to real-life scenarios. This helps learners to internalize what differentiates the restorative approach from punitive, permissive, and neglectful approaches. In an activity called "Build the Nest," learners come to understand how larger social and structural issues contribute to crime through engaging with the Nested Theory of Conflict model by actively "building a nest" of the contributing factors at each social level in relation to a real-life scenario. As you explore the activities outlined in Chapter 8 and implement them in your community, you will undoubtedly begin generating your own creative ideas for how to employ metaphors and models in your design process.

Designing an Activity Step 4: Design the Experience

Once you have your creative framework established, think about how you will facilitate participants' experience of the learning objective. How will you set up and explain the activity? What will they be asked to do? What will be the tone of the activity: is it humorous, reflective, or solemn? Will it be fast-paced, or do you need to modulate speed and create space for silence? How can the activity be intentionally related to real life? How can you create an opportunity to practice a skill in a way that is fun and low stress? How will you help learners draw connections between the immediate learning outcomes and their long-term visions for a more just, equitable world?

Restorative practices fundamentally require a paradigm shift. It is crucial to allow learners the space to discover this new way of thinking for themselves in order to disrupt the conditioned behaviors and thought patterns instilled by the retributive system that is so pervasive in our lives. This is accomplished by facilitating experiences through which learners can undergo a shift in thinking themselves. In order to do this effectively, take time to consider how you will facilitate a meaningful and reflective experience for your learners in each stage of your activity.

Experiential learning activities or games will often involve a mock scenario of a conflict or crime. Writing effective scenarios is key to cultivating a successful learning experience, and having multiple scenarios can help keep the same activities engaging, or lead to discussions highlighting different learning points from the same activity.

In writing a scenario, first revisit your learning objective and consider what sort of discussion you hope to elicit in the group. Next, take the time to reflect on your own life and facilitation experience. The best scenarios are often inspired by real experiences. Writing case studies following each process you facilitate can help provide material for you to teach with later. Or, reflect on your own life. Consider times you experienced conflict or harm or times you caused harm to someone else. Starting with a real experience and changing personally identifying information or overly complex details often results in a scenario that feels authentic.

While designing scenarios, it is also important to pause and check your assumptions and what may be implicitly embedded within the scenario. Has the responsible party been given a name that suggests a certain ethnicity? What about the harmed party? What genders are the characters? Do your scenarios perpetuate destructive stereotypes, or is the scenario a way to engage with and challenge those stereotypes? Intentionally framing a scenario to generate dialogue among learners can be a powerful way to surface and challenge assumptions and shed light on the lived experiences of learners. How will you utilize this opportunity to empower the voices of students from marginalized communities? As the instructor, be prepared to facilitate a respectful dialogue when learners' differing opinions, perspectives, and experiences are brought to the surface.

Designing an Activity Step 5: Design the Debrief

After you have prepared your experiential activity and any required scenarios, the next step is to think about how you will debrief the activity with learners. How can you encourage meaningful conversation, including critical reflection on social issues? Through an effective debrief, learners gain new insight about the meaning of their experience in the activity while integrating new understandings and skills.

The debrief process provides a space where learners can incorporate what has been experienced into their frame of reference and understanding of the world. Through facilitated debriefing, learners begin to see themselves within a web of connectivity that extends beyond the learning space and imagine their role and opportunity to impact larger social systems. When a teacher assumes that learners will integrate new information on their own without a facilitated debrief, they run the risk of providing a diluted learning experience.

An effective debrief should also help learners to understand the connection between the "micro" learning experience and the larger "macro" issues or concepts being explored. Dialoguing about difficult topics—such as structural issues and the role learners play in systems that cause harm—will likely cause tension and discomfort. As the instructor, model embracing this discomfort by courageously facilitating dialogue that upholds the values of respect and responsibility as the group reflects on the underlying issues that have been surfaced.

Conversations about crime scenarios will often provoke more philosophical conversation about the unjust conditions that frequently lead to crime, and the social responsibility necessary to change those conditions. These conversations are infinitely valuable and necessary in order to avoid the often-narrow focus of restorative justice on individual or interpersonal concerns. Cultivating this balance between individual matters and larger structural issues is not an easy task and requires practice, but the potential impact of these dialogues is immense.

Example Debrief Questions for Encouraging Meaningful Reflection

- What was that like for you?
- What did you find easy, and what was more challenging?
- How did the activity change how you think/feel about _____?
- What did you observe in yourself as you practiced this skill?
- How does this activity relate to your lived experience?
- How does this activity help you better understand _____?
- How does this activity relate to your role as a restorative practitioner?

- What will be challenging about implementing this learning in your life/work?
- What is one thing you/we can do to address the issues surfaced through this activity?

Tips for Facilitating an Effective Debrief

- Don't rush it.
- Ensure equal voice in the group.
- Provide validating responses to students' sharing. Reflect back the themes you hear to affirm the wisdom of the group and to help land salient points that convey your learning objectives. Ask follow-up questions to lead students into deeper reflection and inquiry.
- Don't shut down learners' comments as wrong. Instead, dig deeper. Learners may initially respond with resistance, skepticism, or a problematic perception of the concept you have introduced. Rather than shutting down the observation or correcting it, ask the participant to reflect further on the source of the belief or reaction by posing additional respectful, open-ended questions. If you are working with co-facilitators, be prepared to support each other in the case that you receive feedback that is particularly challenging.

Designing an Activity Step 6: Review and Improve Your Experiential Activity

The final step is to review your design and to reflect on the successes and challenges that arise when you use the activity with your group of learners. This creative process involves constant reflection and refinement. As the restorative teaching approach flattens the hierarchy that is often found in teacher-student relationships, you will be a learner yourself at every stage of this process. This way of teaching demands a great deal of attention, skill, and courage.

Because of this demand, the authors recommend finding a group of like-minded trainers and facilitators with whom you can collaborate in the creative process. Through working as a team, you may be able to shed light on each other's blind spots, and offer support through the sometimes-painful process of uncovering previously unidentified biases and assumptions. With the shared goal of designing meaningful, transformative, experiential learning methods, practitioners can share and support the courageous vulnerability that will ultimately lead to a more powerful experience for everyone present.

7.
How to Design an Activity-Based Class or Training

At Longmont Community Justice Partnership's trainings for new volunteer facilitators, our goal is to have participants practice basic facilitation skills. In a group of strangers, participants often become nervous and resistant to taking risks in front of others. As a training team, we designed a daily agenda that uses games to produce an intentional arch: start the morning with relationship building ("See Ya"), facilitate a skills-building game requiring risk and vulnerability at midday ("Curiosity Did Not Harm the Cat" or "Shovel Face"), and close the day with an activity that deepens skills and creates a sense of accomplishment and fun through teamwork ("Out of the Box" or "Race to Reframe").

With this structure, participants are not only more willing to practice facilitating, they also relax and

connect more deeply with each other. As trainers, we model the importance of honoring the serious nature of the work while balancing that with playfulness and not taking ourselves too seriously. We observe participants letting go of concerns about getting everything "right" the first time because they are immersed in the game. Students finish the training as a newly formed community, even more inspired by the potential of restorative justice and their role in it thanks to the friendships and shared sense of purpose they have formed with each other.
—Kathleen McGoey

This chapter offers guidance on how to design a class or training that integrates activity-based, experiential learning. Now that you understand the conceptual frameworks supporting the use of games and activities for teaching restorative practices, have considered how to prepare yourself to facilitate, and have step-by-step instructions for creating your own activity, it is time to address how to incorporate activities into a comprehensive learning experience. Integrating all the recommendations made thus far is a tall order. Assembling the "full package" of your training or class asks you to take a great degree of responsibility in preparation, design, delivery, and self-reflection. The intent that you bring to the design and delivery of the class will have a significant impact on the learners' experiences.

Design and Delivery of a Restorative Learning Experience

Following a sequence of steps will help you design the learning experience as a whole. These steps include establishing a purpose or goal, designing the agenda, and considering how you will deliver or facilitate the learning experience.

Preparing the Class Step 1: Establish a Goal

Take the questions provided in "Designing an Activity Step 2: Identify a Need and Establish a Learning Objective" in Chapter 6 and apply them to the class, workshop, or training day as a whole. What do you want learners to understand or be able to do after the class? Is there a particular phase of the restorative justice process that learners need to practice? Think about one or two specific skill areas where your learners have demonstrated a need for practice and improvement. How can you approach development of those skills through a mix of instruction, experiential learning, and reflection? Consider the conceptual foundations underlying the skills and look for connections that will help you weave together multiple activities to scaffold the learning experience.

Based on the skill areas and knowledge you seek to develop, identify the goal or goals of the comprehensive experience. Some possible goals may include:

- Learners will practice ways to encourage responsibility-taking through affective questions and reflective statements.
- Learners will develop understanding and skills for facilitating a strengths-based agreement in the restorative justice process.
- Learners will deepen their knowledge of the purpose and efficacy of various restorative models and discern when to implement each model.

- Learners will become more aware of the structural and systemic forces affecting individual choice and how to address those in the restorative process.
- Learners will gain insight on the importance of self-regulation and gain experience remaining present when facilitating the restorative justice process.

Continue to reference your goals as you build out the class agenda. This will help you focus and organize the teaching team's efforts.

Preparing the Class Step 2: Design the Agenda

An agenda provides a map for your class or training. The more thought, creativity, and care you employ in writing your agenda, the more prepared you will be to lead a structured and flexible learning experience. The agenda must be clear and relevant for each person responsible for delivery and facilitation. Remember that this agenda will become an invaluable record of what was done. You can return to it immediately following the class in order to debrief the experience and in the future for planning and delivering subsequent classes.

After considering the overarching goals and context of your group, turn your attention to the specific structure of the learning experience. It is important that the pacing and sequence of activities incrementally support learners to take risks and grow at the edge of their comfort zone. Pushing learners into a game they are not ready for, or do not have adequate trust to participate in, may create resistance or cause learners to distance themselves from the group. Begin with a relationship-building activity to help learners connect. Remember, starting with laughter is key. Once relationships are established, introduce games that are more challenging and ask learners to take risks. End with activities that offer an opportunity for learners to apply new skills and synthesize learning. At the end of the class, be observant of the "climate" of the group. Endeavor to conclude the learning experience on a hopeful note that highlights group achievements, connection, or concrete action steps that can be taken outside of class.

In order to help learners make connections between the class content and their own lived experiences, develop a flexible agenda that can be departed from as needed. Intersperse instruction with experiential activities and consider how you will engage with different learning styles: visual, kinesthetic, and auditory.

> Visual learners understand best when information is presented to them visually. Kinesthetic learners integrate new information by using their hands and bodies. Auditory learners need to hear new information.

Be realistic about timing, and only include games or activities when you can allot enough time for a meaningful debrief. Because the debrief is where the gems of reflection and real-life application are shared and integrated, it is the most crucial learning moment and requires the most flexibility. Ideally, your agenda will allow you to be responsive to the students' own inquiries and ideas. While it is always necessary to be aware of time and to keep the class moving, it is also important to attend to learners' real-time learning processes and adapt to what arises, even if that means deviating from your expectations. Keep in mind that in this setting, if learners' discoveries and input produce outcomes that differ from what you expected and challenge you as the facilitator, you are probably doing something right.

There are a few additional questions to consider that will help you to design an effective agenda. These include: Who are the learners and what is their context? What methodologies will be used and what materials are needed? When, where, and how long will the class be? Once a location is identified, consider how that setting will relate to the topics discussed and if it will feel comfortable for all learners. For example, places like police stations, churches, or court buildings may elicit feelings of vulnerability, intimidation, or fear for some students and inhibit the creation of a brave space for participation. How will the class be evaluated? It is never too soon to schedule time for an intentional feedback and debrief session so that learning can be recorded and inform future teaching endeavors.

Preparing the Class Step 3: Teaching as a Team

If you are teaching with others, be intentional about discussing your approach. The entire teaching team should be ready to teach in a way that is congruent with the values of restorative pedagogy. Create a highly relational environment that challenges the traditional classroom hierarchy by setting up opportunities for dialogue between learners and teachers. Teachers should participate in all activities when possible to bring the group closer together and model the concept of learning *with*, upending the concept of teacher as expert. In the agenda, make it clear which teacher has responsibility for facilitating each component and strive to balance the voices being heard. The authors have found it useful to assign the debrief of an activity to a teacher who was not the facilitator of that activity. This allows the teacher leading the debrief to be observant of all participants and catch nuances that the activity facilitator may not have been able to track. The activity facilitator, meanwhile, can shed light on decisions they made or responses they gave during the activity in the debrief.

Be dynamic and model the attitude you wish to see in co-teachers and learners alike. In a restorative learning community, this requires you to bring joy and playfulness as well as reverence and solemnity to the act of teaching. When co-training with youth or people who are new to teaching, build their confidence by letting them know in advance how you will support them. If you have experienced significant conflict or tension with a co-teacher, take measures to clear the air and create shared agreements for how you relate to each other prior to the class, or be ready to name the conflict explicitly with learners and use it as a teaching moment.

Preparing the Class Step 4: Basic Tips for Delivery

From her experience teaching university students, bell hooks notes, "To perform with excellence and grace teachers must be totally present in the moment, totally concentrated and focused. When we are not fully present, when our minds are elsewhere, our teaching is diminished."[1]

> Just as a restorative justice facilitator must be fully present to artfully and effectively lead a process between responsible and harmed individuals, so must a teacher of restorative practices bring their full presence to the responsibility of teaching.

Begin the class by greeting and welcoming learners as they arrive. Be thorough with introductions. The Connection Circle process provides a highly effective way for the group to introduce themselves and to begin forming connections. Share who you are and what gifts and limitations you bring to the topics being covered. This style of introduction will most likely require opening up more than a teacher would in a conventional learning environment. Modeling your own strengths and challenges sets the tone for how learners will be asked to participate, so consider how you can be transparent about your personal experiences from the start. Talk about why you are teaching the class and your relationship to the material, in particular how you understand your own role in systems of power and oppression, and how you see this immediate work as contributing to your dreams for a more just world. Strive to be concise and remember the purpose of this vulnerability is to open the space for learners to do the same.

Following introductions, let learners know what to expect during the class in terms of content and expectations for participation. Provide an overview of the day, explain how to get needs met (breaks, bathroom, food, water), and encourage self-care. Present the goals of the class and establish group norms. Utilize the ground rules of brave spaces as a starting point. One way to flatten teacher-learner hierarchy right away is to co-create these norms, or expectations for participation, collaboratively with learners. This will encourage ownership of the learning experience and ask learners to take responsibility for their own participation.

Describe the style and intent of the class methodology, highlighting the importance of equal voice and learning from each other. Remind learners that they will be asked to apply skills and concepts to their own lives, and the group experience will be enhanced when all voices are heard. Hold learners accountable to this request by engaging with them through questions, validations, and reframing throughout the class. In the interest of equal voice, ask learners to pay attention to how often they are speaking up and when they may need to pause in order to create space for others' contributions.

Review and Improve the Overall Learning Experience

At the end of the class, note your observations about the efficacy of activities and their sequencing. Hold a group debrief with other teachers as soon as possible. Discuss your progress toward your original goal and critically reflect as a team about how learners participated. Begin to brainstorm different activities that could be substituted or created to better reach your goal next time. Based on what you have accomplished, plan how you will track learners' application of the material and provide coaching to sustain integration of new skills. Recognize and celebrate your successes!

8.
Games and Activities for Your Community

This chapter will provide in-depth instructions for facilitating pedagogical games and activities, and how to debrief those experiences with students. The games and activities are organized by different themes and skills that a restorative educator may wish to address with learners. Instructions and print-outs of materials (when applicable) are available at www.restorative teachingtools.com along with additional games and activities.

Read Before Playing: Three Universal Guidelines for Game Facilitation

There are three crucial guidelines to keep in mind that will ultimately determine the efficacy of these games and activities. First, many games allow for rules to be added. Adding rules increases the difficulty of the game and therefore pushes the group towards the edge of their comfort zone and encourages development of new skills. If the game is too easy, it will become boring and could potentially feel like a waste of time to learners. Remember, growth and transformation require discomfort.

Second, if you are providing ongoing training with the same group, work towards having learners contribute to the design and facilitation of the games. This is particularly important when working with young people. Ask youth to write mock scenarios that make the game more relevant to their real-life experiences. Request that youth co-facilitate or even lead the game. The authors have noticed that youth contributions give these games new life and make the games much more fun—and often hilarious—for everyone.

Third, adjust the games to make them inclusive for all learners. If you have differing levels of physical ability in your group that make it difficult to actually "race" in "Race to Reframe," change it so that each group has their own frame and makes an audible sound, or rings a bell, when they have their reframe sentence ready. If there are differing reading levels in the group, read scenarios out loud and use different verbal or kinetic cues to emphasize important points. It is always worth making an effort to modify activities to make them as inclusive as possible!

8.1 Games and Activities to Build Relationships

This section includes instructions for how to facilitate a game to build relationships in a group, going beyond typical "ice breakers" to encourage meaningful connection and highlight the importance of relationship building in restorative processes.

See Ya!

Objective: Students will build relationships, get to know each other, and make connections quickly. Start the day with laughter!

Materials: A list of 5–8 discovery questions. Use the questions below to get started, then create your own.

Instructions: Divide into groups with roughly four people per group. The game facilitator asks one discovery question. Within their small groups, each person shares their answer to that question. After every member of the group has shared their answer, the group quickly decides on the "winner" for that category. For example, the group determines the person with the most siblings, coolest socks, weirdest pet, etc. The group then says, "See ya!" to the winner, and the winner moves on to the next group (in a clockwise direction). Because the discovery questions elicit storytelling and groups may finish answering at different times, the facilitator will need to manage the time and call out when it is time to finish sharing and say "See ya!" to the winner.

Once the "winners" of the round have joined their new groups, the process begins again with the facilitator asking the next discovery question. Plan for at least five rounds, though the number of rounds can vary according to time and group size. To make the game meaningful, questions should be sequenced deliberately. Initial questions should be easy, requiring little risk. As they progress, questions should invite students to take risks to share something more personal. *Note:* While the language of this game may initially seem very competitive, you will see how it unfolds playfully once you get going.

Example Discovery Questions:
- Who has the most siblings?
- Who has the best middle name?
- Who has eaten the strangest food?
- Who has traveled on the coolest form of transportation?
- Who has the most interesting hobby?
- Who has had the weirdest job?
- Who has had the best 1 minute of fame?
- Who has gotten in the most trouble at school?
- Whose current career is most similar to their childhood dream?

Debrief: What is one new or interesting thing you learned about someone else? What did you learn through this activity that relates to restorative practices?

Lesson: Making connections is extremely important when you are facilitating difficult or high-stakes conversations. Realize that each one of us has unique stories and by surfacing these experiences, you can ease tension and help people feel connected.

8.2 Games and Activities to Understand the Restorative Philosophy

This section includes instructions for how to facilitate games and activities to deepen learners' understanding of the restorative philosophy and approach to conflict and wrongdoing.

Social Discipline Window Shuffle

Objective: Students will internalize the restorative approach to conflict, behavior issues, and harm. They will understand and be able to contrast the restorative approach with other approaches.

Materials: Masking tape and paper to create a large Social Discipline Window on the ground in a space where students can gather around. Identical pieces of paper with "not" "to" "for" and "with" written on them. Conflict scenarios that are relevant to your group and their context (i.e., if you are working with school staff, use school-based scenarios that will feel relatable to their work and daily interactions). *Note:* You need four or more students to play this game.

Instructions: Begin by offering a basic introduction to the Social Discipline Window. The Social Discipline Window describes four basic approaches

Reprinted from Ted Wachtel, "Defining Restorative" (illustration: Social Discipline Window), International Institute for Restorative Practices, 2016.

to maintaining social norms and behavioral boundaries.[1] The four approaches are represented as different combinations of high or low control and high or low support. When there is high control (or high expectations of behavior), but low support, this is a punitive or "to" approach. When there is high support, but low control (or low expectations of behavior), this is a permissive or "for" approach. When there is both low support and low control, this is a neglectful or "not" approach. The restorative domain combines both high control (or high expectations of behavior) and high support and is characterized by doing things "with" people, rather than "to" them or "for" them. As you're explaining this conceptual tool, it is helpful to use a simple and relatable scenario from your life so that you can give a quick example of each approach. For example, the authors often use the example of someone we live with not doing the dishes, and describe briefly what neglectful, permissive, punitive, and restorative approaches to that scenario would look like as they describe the model.

Next, divide the group into four teams. Randomly and discretely (so that no one knows what each team has) give each team a piece of paper with the name of one of the quadrants on it ("not," "to," "for," or "with"). After each team has quietly seen which quadrant they have, read a conflict scenario to the entire group. Each team has one minute to work together to formulate a response to the conflict that matches their quadrant (i.e., the "for" team has to come up with a permissive response to the scenario).

When time is up, each team takes a turn to either act out or describe their response to the scenario. Ask the other teams to identify which quadrant the presented response fits in. Ask a representative from the presenting team to stand in that quadrant. Continue until each team has had a chance to share their response. After all four representatives are in their quadrants, discuss each response.

What is the impact of each response? What is problematic about the "to" response? The "for" response? The "not" response? What is effective about the "with" response? How could it be made even more restorative?

Repeat the process with one or two additional scenarios, assigning the "to," "for," "not," and "with" papers to different teams (discretely) before each round so that each team has a chance to practice and internalize multiple approaches and what makes them different.

Debrief: What are the benefits of the "with" approach? As you go about your life, how can you remember to approach issues restoratively? Reflecting on the different areas of your life (work, family, friends, etc.), what is your default response to harm and conflict? How can you use this tool as a mental map to strive to respond more restoratively in each of those contexts? When have you experienced each of these approaches in your life, and what was it like?

Lesson: You can choose to use restorative approaches in all areas of your life. What differentiates a restorative approach from other approaches is that you take time to support another person, while also holding high expectations of their behavior. Accountability and understanding are equally important. It takes practice to achieve this balance and is an ongoing area of development for all of us.

8.3 Skills-Development Games and Activities

The games in this section are pedagogical exercises designed to develop and strengthen specific skills related to facilitating and participating in restorative justice processes. Skills include asking open-ended, affective questions; brainstorming creative ideas for repairing harms; making reflective statements; reframing; understanding needs; and understanding and addressing structural injustices.

8.3.1 Asking Good (Open-Ended, Affective) Questions

The games in this section help students practice asking open-ended (cannot be answered with a simple "yes" or "no"; dig deeper into an experience) and affective (related to emotions, attitudes, or mood) questions. These are essential skills for restorative processes.

Curiosity Did Not Harm the Cat

Objective: Students will practice asking good questions (open-ended, affective) and moving quickly between active listening, speaking, and generating relevant questions. This game's difficulty level can be adjusted according to the skill level of your group.

Materials: None

Instructions: Students sit in one large circle. Person A asks a question (of their choosing) to Person B, who is sitting next to them. Person B responds, then asks a question to the following person. Each subsequent question must be related in some way to the response to the previous question.

Example:

Person A: "What kind of music do you like?"

Person B: "Jazz." *(Turns to next person.)* "What is the last concert you went to?"

Person C: "Rising Appalachia." *(Turns to next person.)* "If you could sing like anyone, who would it be?"

To add a competitive edge, participants may be eliminated if they repeat a question, do not ask a question that relates to the answer they just gave, or if they do not answer the question.

As the game advances, the facilitator will add more rules.

Additional Rules:
1. You must ask the question with a tone of curiosity.
2. Open-ended questions only.
3. Affective questions only.
4. Person A must respond with a reflective statement after Person B answers the question, and so on.

Note: To remain clear and focused as the facilitator, it may be helpful to stay out of this game and just facilitate. If you have more than one teacher present, ask other teachers to participate while you facilitate.

Debrief: What was that like for you? What was challenging? What did you notice about asking different kinds of questions? What did you notice about making the transition from answering the question to asking the next one? How does this apply to your role as a facilitator or restorative practitioner?

Lesson: This game simulates the restorative justice facilitator's role and the focus required to practice active listening and forming questions (and reflections) based on what you hear. While a facilitator is typically following the overarching questions of restorative justice (What happened? Who was affected? What needs to happen to repair the harms and make things right?), they have the opportunity to listen for and elicit deeper reflection by asking additional questions or responding with reflective statements. This game creates a fun, low-pressure way to practice that essential skill.

Shovel Face[2]

Objective: Students practice active listening, asking open-ended follow-up questions, and using reflective statements when someone has just shared something that is deeply personal.

Materials: None

Instructions: Students sit in one large circle. Person A asks a "primary" thought-provoking question of Person B, seated to their right. Person B will answer the question in 1–3 sentences (remind participants that the focus of the game is not on storytelling, but Person B does need to provide enough information to allow Person A to ask a relevant follow-up question). Person A responds by asking one open-ended, follow-up question. Person B answers that question. Person A listens, and then asks one more open-ended, follow-up question to probe deeper into the experience of Person B. After Person B responds to the second follow-up question, that pair is complete. Person A says "thank you" to Person B, and the game progresses to Person C, who is seated to the right of Person B. Person C will share their brief response to the same primary question asked of Person B. They will repeat the same exchange, with Person B asking two follow-up questions of Person C, thanking them to conclude their conversation, and then the game moves on to Person D's response to the primary question and exchange with Person C. Go all the way around the circle so that eventually every person has answered the same primary question, and every person has listened and asked two follow-up questions.

You may increase the difficulty of the game by adding rules as the game progresses, such as:

- The question must be open-ended *and* affective (related to emotions, attitudes, or mood).
- Before asking a follow-up question, you must make a reflective statement that seeks to capture the content, emotion, and/or meaning of what the speaker shared.

Remind students that it is acceptable to pause and allow for silence before asking a question. While it may be a new or uncomfortable practice, a silent pause can be very powerful. Tell students in advance that you may need to interject during the game to help them rework a closed question.

Example:

Primary Question (Person A):	"What is the most significant learning experience of your life and what did you learn?"
Person B:	"The most significant learning experience of my life was when my daughter was born. I learned how deeply I can love and that I'm a lot stronger than I thought I was."
Person A:	"What was it about the experience that showed you how strong you are?"
Person B:	"She was born at home, and I felt proud that my body and mind could find a place of peace and fearlessness through an unmedicated birth. I felt like, through the experience, I tapped into a part of myself that I didn't know was there before."

Person A:	"How has it impacted your life to be in touch with this new part of yourself?"
Person B:	"It made me feel more ready to be a mother, knowing that strength was there. Now I can connect with that part of myself when I need to feel strong."
Person A:	"Thank you for sharing."
Person C:	"The most significant learning experience of my life was when my sister got sick. It felt like I had to become an adult overnight, but it taught me how important family is."
Person B:	*(Asks open-ended follow-up question.)*

Debrief: When the activity is complete, invite everyone to stand up, take some deep breaths, and move their bodies. Gentle shaking is an effective way to clear a heavy or stressful experience. After providing space for self-care, ask: How was that for you? What did you do that helped you form questions that elicited more information from the speaker? What helps you stay present when facilitating an intense moment?

Lesson: As a restorative justice facilitator, you will often surface stories and information from participants'

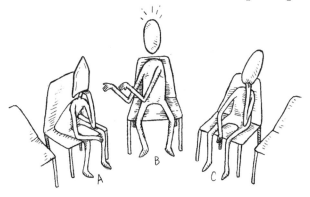

lives that reveal something deeply personal and may provoke a strong emotional response in you. It is difficult to predict when this will happen, what will be shared, and how it will affect you and others present. Practicing being present and responding in the brave space of a game gives you the opportunity to learn about your own reactions and practice self-regulating to remain effective as an impartial facilitator.

8.3.2 Creative Ideas to Repair Harms

Common Everyday Objects

Objective: This is a great game for teaching creative brainstorming while coming up with agreement items. It demonstrates the imaginative power of groups working together and thinking outside the box. It also encourages detachment from the final outcome and creates an environment where no one's idea is turned down.

Materials: One "common everyday object" per group. Objects can be *anything*: a coffee cup, straw, pencil, paperclip, fork, etc.

Instructions: Divide students into groups of 4–8 people. You need to have at least two groups. The more groups you have, the longer the game will take. Give each group a different "common everyday object," and instruct them to designate one member as the scribe. The groups will have two minutes to brainstorm every function their object could be used for, except its intended purpose (i.e., imagine everything that can be done with a pen other than writing). Everyone in the group contributes to brainstorming as many ideas as possible, and the scribe records *all* ideas. You cannot repeat different versions of the same idea (i.e., the pen cannot be used as "1. A straw" *and* "2. To drink with"). The facilitator starts and stops the clock, adding a countdown at the end to increase the intensity and fun. The facilitator then goes group by group, asking the scribe to share what their object is, and to read off all the ideas they listed. The facilitator plays the part of the judge and rules out any repetitions or anything too close to the object's intended use. The group with the most approved ideas wins!

Debrief: What did you notice about brainstorming in a group? How did ideas evolve? Did anyone hold back something they were thinking? Why? How does this relate to brainstorming agreement items in a restorative process?

Lesson: Through healthy competition and playfulness, this game gives learners a taste of what can happen when every person contributes to brainstorming agreements in a restorative process. It creates a spirit of "yes and," which builds momentum and highlights how unrestricted group brainstorming draws out more creative, inventive ideas from each individual. Students learn that even if they feel shy or insecure about their own ideas, they are valuable to share as they will often stimulate more contributions from others.

Out of the Box
Objective: Students will practice brainstorming and finalizing creative, strengths-based agreement items

that are SMART (Specific, Measurable, Achievable, Related, Timely) for restorative justice processes.

Materials: Tape to draw a large "box" for each team on the ground (or, if you happen to have large boxes or bins that a team of 4–7 people could stand in and if the group is familiar enough with each other to feel comfortable being that close, this is an entertaining setup and intensifies the physical experience of the game), a notepad and pen for each team, a mock restorative justice case scenario, and a description of the responsible person's strengths and interests. *Optional:* List these strengths and interests on a poster that is visible to all participants.

Note: This game is easier to lead with a co-facilitator. One facilitator leads the game, and the other acts as the "judge."

Instructions: Divide participants into teams of 4–7 people. All members of each team will stand inside their own box made out of tape on the floor (or an actual box). The size of the box should require the team members to stand close to each other to help create intensity and increase motivation to get out. You may want to begin by reviewing the SMART (Specific, Measurable, Achievable, Related to repairing the harm, Timely) criteria for agreement items as a group.

The facilitator then explains: "I am going to share a case scenario and the responsible person's strengths. Each team will work together to write agreement items that are creative, strengths-based, and SMART that could potentially be used in a contract to repair harm. Here's the catch: your agreement item must be an 'out of the box' idea, meaning it *cannot* be any one of the four most common agreement items: apology letter, poster, PowerPoint, and community service hours. When your team has an idea ready to share, raise your hand and shout 'Repair!' (or another word that has meaning for your group). I will call on you to read your idea out loud. The other groups should pause and listen. The idea must be read in one continuous sentence and clearly have all the elements of SMART. If I accept the item you described because it has fit all the SMART criteria,[3] the person who voiced that item will step out of the box and stand to the side, away from their group. That person is no longer participating in the game (but can certainly cheer on their teammates). If I reject the item, you can continue working on it, but another group can also 'steal' that idea and try to make it fit the criteria. The goal is to be the first team to get all members out of the box."

> Adjust the "four most common agreement items" according to your context! If the community you are working with tends to overly rely on certain agreement items, you can make those part of the box and push participants to use their creative capacity to come up with different creative ideas.

The facilitator needs to be prepared to listen to each proposed agreement item to determine in the moment if it fits all criteria. If you are working with a co-trainer, share responsibilities and ask them to be the judge. Once a teammate is outside the box, they cannot make suggestions. The first team to get all teammates out of the box wins. Depending on group size, this game may require substantial time to complete. Plan for at least 30 minutes. If you don't have enough time to run the game through completion, stop it with enough time to synthesize learning and debrief.

Note: This game can be a little wild and chaotic at first, and that's part of the fun! The facilitator must orchestrate the game, tracking when each team is ready with an idea and indicating which team has the floor, making sure that teams are taking turns. This requires a facilitator who is ready to think on their feet and manage a lot of activity. Recruit a good co-trainer to help you facilitate the first time, don't take yourself too seriously, and don't give up!

Debrief: Ask the last person who was left in the box: How was it different brainstorming ideas with a big group versus alone? Ask everyone: How did your group work together to create agreement item ideas? What got your creativity going? What did you notice when you couldn't rely on the four most common agreement items?

Lesson: When we think "outside the box" and brainstorm together, we are able to come up with more creative ideas to repair harms. Students learn about the importance of making an agreement idea SMART.

8.3.3 Reflective Statements

Mirror Mirror

Objective: Students learn about the importance of reflective statements and will practice making reflective statements in a low-stress, fun environment.

Materials: A soft ball or other item that can be safely and easily tossed around a circle.

Instructions: Start by offering a review of reflective statements by asking students, "What is a reflective statement?" (Answer: A statement reflecting the content, emotion, and/or meaning of what the speaker shared.) Talk about how once you have asked an open-ended question and heard the response, a reflective statement is a great way to show you are listening, make the speaker feel heard, and give them a chance to clarify if there is a misunderstanding. You may ask for examples from the group, or provide examples of reflective statements. For example:

Speaker says: "Ever since then, things with my mom really aren't good. Like, she doesn't trust me to hang out with my friends or do anything, so we fight a lot."

Reflective Statement: "It sounds like the damaged trust with your mom is really impacting your relationship with her."

Ask students to reflect on why they think it would be helpful to use a reflective statement. They may mention that reflective statements show you are listening, show you care about the experience or emotion and are not judging it, build trust and relationship, and give you the chance to check your understanding.

After the review, instruct students to stand in one large circle. You will start holding the ball and will ask an opening question. For example, "What is the last movie you saw and how did it make you feel?" Toss the ball to someone else (Person A) in the circle. Person A answers the question and then tosses it to another person (Person B) in the circle who makes a reflective statement based on what they just heard. Person B then answers the original question and throws the ball to another person (Person C) who makes a reflective statement about Person B's answer, then answers the question themself, and throws the ball to the next person. The game continues on until every person in the circle has made a reflective statement and answered the question.

Note: Sometimes the reflection will not accurately capture the meaning of the original speaker's statement. Explain to learners how an inaccurate reflection can be used as an opportunity for greater clarification. During the game, ask learners to speak up in the moment if/when this happens. For example, if Person B's reflection doesn't resonate with Person A, Person A can ask for the ball back to clarify, then Person B can make a second attempt at reflecting what they heard.

Example:

Facilitator:	"What is the last movie you saw, and how did it make you feel and why?" *(Tosses the ball to Person A.)*
Person A:	"I saw *Remember the Titans,* and it made me feel inspired, because I remembered some of the adults who influenced me when I was younger." *(Tosses the ball to Person B.)*
Person B:	"It sounds like watching that movie was powerful because it reminded you of important people from your past. I saw *Titanic,* and it made me feel frustrated. Why didn't Rose share that floating door with Jack?" *(Tosses the ball to Person C.)*
Person C:	"It sounds like it was more irritating than tragic for you because Jack's death seemed avoidable. I saw *The Sixth Sense* for the first time and was kind of disappointed that someone had ruined the ending for me." *(Tosses the ball to Person D. Games continues on.)*

Debrief: How was it coming up with reflective statements on the spot? When your answer was reflected by someone, how did it feel? Why are reflective statements an important part of the restorative justice process?

Lesson: Reflective statements help us to feel connected and heard while also giving us a chance to check our understanding of someone else's statement. Sometimes a reflective statement can be even more effective than another question in encouraging someone to open up!

8.3.4 Reframing

Race to Reframe

Objective: Students will learn and practice the important facilitation skill of reframing.

Materials: A picture frame (a real one is best, but a frame cut out of paper will work) that is large enough to frame someone's head and a list of statements to reframe. *Optional:* Notepads and pens.

Note: This game is easier to lead with a co-facilitator. One facilitator leads the game, and the other acts as the "judge."

Instructions: You may need to begin by offering a review of the skill of reframing. A "reframe" is a modified reflective statement in which the facilitator restates what has just been said by one party in a way that can be received by the other party without them becoming defensive or reactive. This may involve replacing destructive words and phrasing with constructive words and phrasing or identifying underlying needs. Commonly identified needs are those involving basic survival (food, water, shelter, clothing, etc.) and psychological needs (safety/security, love/belonging, friendship/family, being respected/self-respect, etc.). Reframing is done with a spirit of curiosity and respect, leaving room for the speaker to affirm or clarify.

Example:

Speaker: "I can't stand my teacher. She never pays attention to what other people think."

Facilitator: "It sounds like you don't feel heard."

Divide students into 2–4 teams (depending on group size), and instruct the teams to line up by the wall on one side of the room. Give the teams a few minutes to pick team names (just for fun) and record them on a whiteboard or large paper where you will keep score. The facilitator stands by a frame (real or made of paper) large enough to frame someone's head, which is located about 6 meters away from the teams. The other trainer is the "judge" and stands by the whiteboard. The facilitator reads aloud one statement in need of reframing. It may be helpful to have a team scribe jot down the sentence that needs to be reframed, or you can provide the sentence on a poster or screen for a visual aid. Students discuss the statement with their teams and create an appropriate reframe sentence. As soon as a team has agreed on a reframe sentence, a representative from that team will "race" to put their head in the frame, then share their reframe response out loud. The first team to have a representative reach the frame will be the first team to share their response. Other team representatives can race to the frame and form a line to be the next to speak.

The judge will either approve or deny the reframe attempt. If it is approved, the team will be awarded 4 points for the round. If it is denied, the team representative will return to their team to rework the reframe sentence. The next team representative to reach the frame will be given an opportunity to share their reframe.

- The first team to share an approved reframe receives 4 points
- The second team to share an approved reframe receives 3 points
- The third team to share an approved reframe receives 2 points
- The fourth team to share an approved reframe receives 1 point

The game repeats for a total of four rounds, with four different statements in need of a reframe being read to the group.

Example Statements in Need of Reframing:

Statement 1: "I'm so tired of getting in trouble. I'm always getting blamed for things."

Statement 2: "Now she is a thief. I can't trust her in the house anymore."

Statement 3: "I see these punks in the street at night, and I can't even leave the house."

Statement 4: "She has been treating me like sh** all year. She had it coming."

After the final round, points are tallied, and the winning team is announced. This game should be modified depending on the group's skill level and context for working together. If your group of learners is ready for it, create a list of statements that start off pretty low-impact and increase in offensiveness. In this case, it is important to inform participants ahead of time that you have intentionally chosen statements that may be triggering. Remind participants that in a restorative process, such comments might require a facilitator not only to reframe, but also to revisit ground rules about respect and safety. Accomplishing this also asks individuals to become aware of their own triggers and use self-regulation techniques. Another possible modification is to add nuance to the judge's criteria. Was the reframe clearly delivered with a nonjudgmental tone? In addition to replacing destructive words or sentiment, does the reframe identify an underlying need?

105

Debrief: What was challenging about reframing? What made it easier? What strategies did you use to think objectively about the reframe without getting too emotionally escalated or evaluative? Discuss reframe responses as a group. What was the impact of coming up with a reframe under time pressure? How did this activity relate to your role as a restorative practitioner?

Lesson: Reframing is one of the most difficult and important skills for facilitators to master. Being able to reframe respectfully allows you to diffuse tense moments in a pre-conference or conference and move the parties towards mutual understanding and respect. Practice this skill in your own life by taking time to mentally identify the needs behind hurtful statements you hear.

8.3.5 Understanding Needs

Build the House

Objective: Students will understand how unmet needs often lead to harmful behavior and also how harmful behavior creates needs. Students will be introduced to the *Te Whare Tapa Whā* framework for understanding human needs.

Materials: Four copies of a statement from a responsible party and the four walls of the *Te Whare Tapa Whā* (teh FAH-ray TAH-pah FAH) model that fit together to make a house that can be constructed at the end of the activity. These should be printed on cardstock. For a printable PDF of the *Te Whare Tapa Whā* house, visit www.restorativeteachingtools.com.

Instructions: Introduce the activity by reminding students that restorative justice looks at incidents of harm through a different lens than the conventional criminal justice system. One important element the restorative justice process seeks to uncover is: what are the needs that participants have? These could be unmet needs that led to the negative behavior or needs that are a result of the harm caused.

Often, Maslow's Hierarchy of Needs is employed as a tool for understanding these basic human needs, but the *Te Whare Tapa Whā* model provides an even more relevant framework for restorative practices.

Te Whare Tapa Whā is a Māori framework for understanding health and well-being. *Te Whare Tapa Whā* portrays four dimensions of well-being as four walls, or sides, of a house. If one of the dimensions is missing or damaged, the entire structure (representing the person) will become unbalanced or unwell.

The four dimensions are:

Taha wairua (TAha WAI-ru-ah):	Spiritual well-being
Taha tinana (TAha TEE-nah-nah):	Physical well-being
Taha whanau (TAha FAH-no):	Social well-being
Taha hinengaro (TAha heh-neng-aro):	Mental and emotional well-being

These aspects of an individual's health are deeply interconnected. For example, when someone's mental health is suffering, their physical, spiritual, and social health also all suffer. This is important for us to understand because, ultimately, restorative processes are concerned with achieving well-being.

Once students have been introduced to the *Te Whare Tapa Whā* concept, divide them into four teams. Assign each team one wall of the *Te Whare Tapa Whā* model and give them the printout (preferably on cardstock or heavyweight paper) of that wall. Next, read an example statement from a responsible party (something you might hear during a pre-conference meeting) to the whole group.

Example Statement:
"It's just not fair. I only stole the clothing because I had an interview coming up and nothing to wear. I'm sick of working at that fast food joint. I can't support my family on that money, and I just can't stand it there. Every day is the same. The interview was for a marketing role. I've always thought I would be great at that! Then I could feel like I'm actually doing something. Now I have this court date, and this is hanging over me and my family. Forget about the new job. There is no way they will trust a thief."

Give a written copy of the statement to each of the four groups so they can revisit it during the exercise. Then, give the teams ten minutes to talk through the issue and identify all the needs related to their side of the house that may be involved in the scenario. These could be needs that led to the behavior or needs that now exist as a result of the behavior. Instruct the groups to write the needs they identify directly on their wall.

After ten minutes, have each group share their list of needs with the larger group. After each group has spoken, ask one person from each group to come to the middle of the circle with their wall so that they can build the house together. The activity will end with a collaboratively constructed four-walled house in the middle of the circle with the wide range of needs relevant to the scenario written on all sides.

Debrief: Are there any needs that surprised you? What additional understanding did you gain from looking at the needs in these different categories? How is the *Te Whare Tapa Whā* model relevant in restorative justice? Now, seeing all these needs, what ideas do you have about what could happen next?

Lesson: When we understand the needs that led to a behavior and the needs that have arisen from the

harm caused, we are more able to facilitate a process that fully repairs harm and ensures that the behavior is not repeated. Having a model like *Te Whare Tapa Whā* can help us to understand the range of human needs involved and to explore those components with learners.

8.3.6 Understanding and Addressing Structural Injustices

Build the Nest

Objective: Students will understand how structural injustices contribute to crime and will think about ways to address these issues restoratively.

Materials: You will need to create a large replica of Máire Dugan's Nested Model of Conflict on the floor using string and tape (see next page). Label each level of conflict in the model. You will also need blank paper "sticks" that students can write on. Materials for this game can be downloaded from www.restorative teachingtools.com.

Instructions: Begin by explaining Máire Dugan's Nested Model of Conflict, using a story to illustrate. The authors like to borrow the story that Máire Dugan uses in her article.[4]

Story Summary:
> There was a fight on high school grounds between two groups of white and black teenage male students. The fight started because white students had arrived on campus wearing jackets with Confederate flags on them. No one

was seriously physically injured in the fight, but there was emotional harm to those involved in the fight and the wider community.

Note that a standard restorative justice process may repair the interpersonal relationships between the teenage boys involved in the fight, but is that enough in this case? There are clearly bigger issues in the community that contributed to the fight taking place in the first place. This specific conflict between individuals is a manifestation of deeper societal conflict, structural violence, and historical harm.

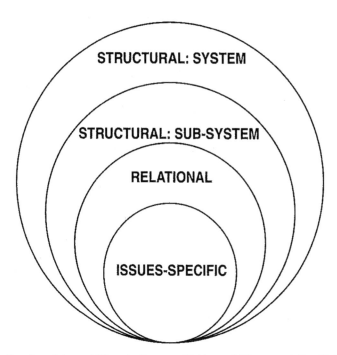

Reprinted from Máire A. Dugan, "A Nested Theory of Conflict" (illustration: A Nested Model of Conflict), *A Leadership Journal: Women in Leadership—Sharing the Vision, Volume 1,* 1996.

Máire Dugan's Nested Theory of Conflict provides a framework for understanding the interrelated types of conflict in a community. Go through each level of the nest with students, discussing how they relate to the example story. Reference the large replica of the model on the floor as you move through each level of conflict.

- *Issue-Specific Conflict* occurs between individuals or groups and the source is one or more specific issues. Ask students, what is the Issue-Specific Conflict in this story? (In this example, it is the wearing of the Confederate flag and the resulting fight.)
- *Relational Conflict* is conflict that emerges from problems having to do with the interaction patterns of the parties involved in the conflict and their feelings toward each other. The relational problem is the source of the conflict, not just the specific issue. Ask students, what is the Relational Conflict in this story? (In this example, it is likely a lack of connection, friendship, and opportunities for respectful interaction between these two groups of students.)
- At this point, it is helpful to skip past Structural: Sub-System Conflict and explain Structural: System Conflict (the outer most layer of the nest) first. *Structural: System Conflict* is conflict that emerges from inequities that are built into social systems. For example, racism, sexism, classism, homophobia, etc. Ask students, what is the System Conflict in this story? As a group, discuss racism in the wider social system as well as a history of slavery, discrimination, and social inequity.

- Next, return to explaining *Structural: Sub-System Conflict*, which is how the rules, procedures, and traditions of particular social organizations manifest System Conflict, often as a result of internalized and institutional oppression. Ask students, what is the Sub-System Conflict in this story? Discuss as a group the ways racism shows up in the rules, procedures, and traditions of the school. Teachers may be more likely to label students of color as "trouble-makers" and punish them more severely for the same behaviors displayed by white students. People of color (and other marginalized groups) are under-represented in history books, literature, etc. There is also often unaddressed racist history within schools (segregation, naming buildings after racist individuals, etc.).

Ensure that the group has a basic understanding of the Nested Model of Conflict, and then divide students into three equal-sized groups. Assign each group a level of conflict from the model: Relational, Sub-System, and System (the Issue-Specific Conflict will be identified by the group as a whole). Read a new scenario to the group and together determine the Issue-Specific Conflict. Then explain that each group is responsible for identifying the relevant factors related to their level of conflict for the scenario. Give each group a stack of paper "sticks" and instruct them to write each factor they identify on a stick.

Example Scenario:
    At a local high school, someone created a private group on an online social media platform for male students wherein several boys swapped

naked or provocative pictures of girls without their consent. Most of the girls in the pictures also attend the school.

Give the groups ten minutes to discuss their level of conflict and to write relevant factors on their sticks. Next, bring students back together and give each of the three groups a chance to share what they discussed. As they name each relevant factor they identified, they should lay the corresponding "stick" down in their level of the nest model on the floor. In this way, the groups are co-constructing a full picture of the nest and all the contributing conflicts related to the specific issue.

Begin with the Relational Conflict group. For this example scenario, they may mention factors such as male and female students objectifying each other because they do not see each other as people, or being able to degrade and disrespect each other because they have little opportunity to have meaningful conversations that challenge stereotypes, assumptions, and biases.

Next, move on to the Structural: Sub-System Conflict group. They may mention a "boys-will-be-boys" attitude, teachers who allow microaggressions and disrespectful jokes on the part of male students, dress codes that target only female students, and other Sub-System factors likely at play in the school.

Finally, move on to the Structural: System Conflict group. They will likely mention issues such as sexism and misogyny in wider society and the media, sexual purity narratives, and the effects of pornography among others.

Allow adequate time to discuss each level of the nest as you move from group to group, ensuring a depth of understanding of how the specific issue is nested in these larger layers of conflict.

Debrief: Having built this nest together, and seeing the true complexity of the issue and how it is a manifestation of greater, more-entrenched societal conflict, what are some outcomes that would address these larger topics? How can we use restorative practices to address these systemic societal issues? How does understanding conflict in this nested way change

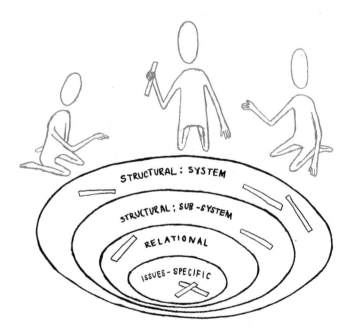

your understanding of restorative justice? How will this aid you as a restorative practitioner?

Lesson: Crime and other forms of misbehavior cannot be understood as isolated incidents, but rather need to be understood as embedded in a wider nest of structural injustices and deeply rooted social inequity. As restorative practitioners, we cannot truly repair harm until we understand and seek to address the larger systemic and historic forces at play.

Notes

Chapter 1: Introduction

1. David Dyck, "Reaching Toward a Structurally Responsive Training and Practice of Restorative Justice," in *Handbook of Restorative Justice*, ed. Dennis Sullivan and Larry Tifft (New York: Routledge, 2008), 527.
2. Fania Davis, *The Little Book of Race and Restorative Justice: Black Lives, Healing, and US Social Transformation* (New York: Good Books, 2019), 35.
3. Davis, *The Little Book of Race and Restorative Justice*, 44.
4. Ibid., 44–45.

Chapter 2: Restorative Pedagogy

1. Parts of Chapters Two, Three, and Four were previously published in Lindsey Pointer and Kathleen McGoey, "Teaching Restorative Practices through Games: An Experiential and Relational Restorative Pedagogy," *The International Journal of Restorative Justice* 2, no. 1 (2019).
2. John Luckner and Reldan Nadler, *Processing the Experience: Strategies to Enhance and Generalize Learning* (Dubuque, Iowa: Kendall/Hunt Publishing Company, 1992), 12.
3. Paulo Freire, *Pedagogy of the Oppressed* (New York: Continuum, 1970/1993), 53.
4. Belinda Hopkins, "Restorative Justice as Social Justice," *Nottingham Law Journal* 21 (2012): 125.
5. Howard Zehr, *The Little Book of Restorative Justice, Revised and Updated* (New York: Good Books, 2015), 48. Gerry Johnstone and Daniel Van Ness, "The

117

Meaning of Restorative Justice," in *Handbook of Restorative Justice*, ed. Gerry Johnstone and Daniel Van Ness (Portland, Oregon: Willan Publishing, 2007), 17. Kristina Llewellyn and Jennifer Llewellyn, "A Restorative Approach to Learning: Relational Theory as Feminist Pedagogy in Universities," in *Feminist Pedagogy in Higher Education: Critical Theory and Practice*, ed. Tracy Penny Light, Jane Nicholas, and Renée Bondy (Waterloo, Ontario: Wilfrid Laurier University Press, 2015), 16. Kay Pranis, "Restorative Values," in *Handbook of Restorative Justice*, ed. Gerry Johnstone and Daniel Van Ness (Portland, Oregon: Willan Publishing, 2007), 65–66.
6. Freire, *Pedagogy of the Oppressed*.
7. Ibid., 61.
8. bell hooks, *Teaching to Transgress: Education as the Practice of Freedom* (New York: Routledge, 1994), 8.
9. Dyck, "Reaching Toward a Structurally Responsive Training and Practice of Restorative Justice," 527.
10. Dorothy Vaandering, "The Significance of Critical Theory for Restorative Justice in Education," *Review of Education, Pedagogy, and Cultural Studies* 32, no. 2 (2010): 168.
11. Barb Toews, "Toward a Restorative Justice Pedagogy: Reflections on Teaching Restorative Justice in Correctional Facilities," *Contemporary Justice Review* 16, no. 1 (2013): 6.

Chapter 3: Experiential Learning and Restorative Justice
1. Luckner and Nadler, *Processing the Experience: Strategies to Enhance and Generalize Learning*, 3.
2. Michael J. Gilbert, Mara Schiff, and Rachel H. Cunliffe, "Teaching Restorative Justice: Developing a Restorative Andragogy for Face-to-Face, Online and Hybrid Course Modalities," *Contemporary Justice Review* 16, no. 1 (2013): 55.
3. Llewellyn and Llewellyn, "A Restorative Approach to Learning: Relational Theory as Feminist Pedagogy in Universities," 19.

4. Jeremy A. Rinker and Chelsey Jonason, "Restorative Justice as Reflective Practice and Applied Pedagogy on College Campuses," *Journal of Peace Education* 11, no. 2 (2014): 165.

5. Barbara A. Carson and Darrol Bussler, "Teaching Restorative Justice to Education and Criminal Justice Majors," *Contemporary Justice Review* 16, no. 1 (2013): 142.

6. Kristi Holsinger, "Teaching to Make a Difference," *Feminist Criminology* 3, no. 4 (2008): 332.

Chapter 4: Building a Restorative Learning Community

1. Christopher Marshall, "The Evolution and Meaning of the Restorative City Ideal: An Introductory Essay," (unpublished, Victoria University of Wellington, 2016).

2. Jennifer J. Llewellyn and Brenda Morrison, "Deepening the Relational Ecology of Restorative Justice," *The International Journal of Restorative Justice* 1, no. 3 (2018): 346–47.

3. Howard Zehr, *Changing Lenses: A New Focus for Crime and Justice* (Harrisonburg, Virginia: Herald Press, 1990), 268.

4. Davis, *The Little Book of Race and Restorative Justice*, 18.

5. Kristina R. Llewellyn and Christina Parker, "Asking the 'Who': A Restorative Purpose for Education Based on Relational Pedagogy and Conflict Dialogue," *The International Journal of Restorative Justice* 1, no. 3 (2018): 401.

6. bell hooks, *Teaching Community: A Pedagogy of Hope* (New York: Routledge, 2003), 109.

7. Ibid.

8. Lindsey Pointer, "Justice Performed: The Normative, Transformative, and Proleptic Dimensions of the Restorative Justice Ritual," (PhD dissertation, Victoria University of Wellington, 2019).

9. Victor Turner, *The Ritual Process: Structure and Anti-Structure* (Chicago: Aldine Publishing Company, 1969).

10. Victor Turner, *From Ritual to Theatre: The Human Seriousness of Play* (New York: Performing Arts Journal Publications, 1982).

11. Walter Crist, Alex de Voogt, and Anne-Elizabeth Dunn-Vaturi, "Facilitating Interaction: Board Games as Social Lubricants in the Ancient Near East," *Oxford Journal of Archaeology* 35, no. 2 (2016): 179.

12. J. Tuomas Harviainen and Andreas Lieberoth, "Similarity of Social Information Processes in Games and Rituals: Magical Interfaces," *Simulation & Gaming* 43, no. 4 (2012): 529.

13. J. Tuomas Harviainen, "Ritualistic Games, Boundary Control, and Information Uncertainty," *Simulation & Gaming* 43, no. 4 (2012): 523–33.

Chapter 5: Preparing to Teach

1. Carl Rogers, "The Necessary and Sufficient Conditions of Therapeutic Personality Change," *Journal of Consulting Psychology* 21, no. 2 (1957): 95–103. doi: 10.1037/h0045357

2. Annie O'Shaughnessy, "Transforming Teaching and Learning through Mindfulness-Based Restorative Practices," in *Getting More out of Restorative Practices in Schools*, ed. Margaret Thorsborne, Nancy Riestenberg, and Gillean McCluskey (London: Jessica Kingsley Publishers, 2019), 149.

3. Toews, "Toward a Restorative Justice Pedagogy: Reflections on Teaching Restorative Justice in Correctional Facilities," 21–23.

4. Toews, "Toward a Restorative Justice Pedagogy," 22.

5. Ibid.

6. Ibid., 23.

7. Brian Arao and Kristi Clemens, "From Safe Spaces to Brave Spaces: A New Way to Frame Dialogue Around Diversity and Social Justice," in *The Art of Effective Facilitation: Reflections from Social Justice Educators*, ed. Lisa M. Landreman (Sterling, VA: Stylus, 2013), 143–148.

8. Ibid., 142.
9. hooks, *Teaching Community: A Pedagogy of Hope*, 132.
10. Ibid., 28–29.
11. Ibid., 27–30, 64.
12. Daniel Siegel, *The Developing Mind: How Relationships and the Brain Interact to Shape Who We Are*, 2nd ed. (New York: Guilford Press, 2012), 281–283.
13. hooks, *Teaching Community: A Pedagogy of Hope*, 143.

Chapter 6: How to Design an Experiential Activity for Teaching Restorative Practices

1. Edward Taylor, "Transformative Learning Theory," *New Directions for Adult and Continuing Education* 2008, no. 119 (2008): 13. doi: 10.1002/ace.301

Chapter 7: How to Design an Activity-Based Class or Training

1. hooks, *Teaching Community: A Pedagogy of Hope*, 14.

Chapter 8: Games and Activities for Your Community

1. Ted Wachtel, "Defining Restorative" (illustration: Social Discipline Window), International Institute for Restorative Practices, 2016, accessed June 17, 2019, https://www.iirp.edu/defining-restorative/social-discipline-window.
2. Note on the name: Laura Snider and Ken Keusenkothen, dear friends and colleagues of the authors, introduced us to the concept of the "shovel face," in which the facilitator's expression and body language change as they begin to "dig deeper" into the speaker's story.
3. Determine the difficulty level of the game based on your program's criteria for agreement items and skill level of the group.
4. Maire Dugan, "A Nested Theory of Conflict," *A Leadership Journal: Women in Leadership—Sharing the Vision* 1, no. 1(1996): 9–20, https://emu.edu/cjp/docs/Dugan_Maire_Nested-Model-Original.pdf.

Acknowledgments

This Little Book has grown out of our collaboration with many exceptional restorative practitioners. In particular, we have been inspired by the creative genius and dedication of our friends and colleagues, Laura Snider, Ken Keusenkothen, and Karin Higgins. Thank you to our communities at Longmont Community Justice Partnership in Colorado and the Diana Unwin Chair in Restorative Justice at Victoria University of Wellington in New Zealand. These incredible teams have supported us and encouraged our growth as practitioners, trainers, and researchers.

We recognize and appreciate the responsible parties, harmed parties, volunteers, police, and community stakeholders who we engage with in restorative processes. These individuals drive our inspiration to improve restorative justice practices by developing more engaged and transformative learning experiences. We would also like to honor indigenous peoples from around the world who innovated restorative approaches for building healthy, connected communities, as well as the many practitioners, activists, and scholars who we continue to learn so much from.

We also want to extend our gratitude to our editor, Barb Toews, who offered helpful feedback and was an absolute joy to work with, and Colleen McGuire, who provided the excellent illustrations in Chapter 8.

Finally, we would like to thank our families and friends, whose care, enthusiasm, and belief in us and our work have made this project possible.

About the Authors

Lindsey Pointer is a restorative practices educator, researcher, and practitioner. She has a PhD in Restorative Justice from Victoria University of Wellington in New Zealand, where she helped design and implement the Restorative University initiative. Lindsey is a former Fulbright Fellow and Rotary Global Grant recipient who is passionate about experimenting with new applications of restorative principles and processes and understanding how restorative practices work to transform communities. She has worked internationally with communities in a range of contexts to support the implementation of restorative practices in an engaged, responsive, and fun way. She currently lives in Colorado.

Kathleen McGoey is the executive director of Longmont Community Justice Partnership (LCJP), a nonprofit that implements community- and schools-based restorative practices programs and training. Kathleen's previous experience leading a peacebuilding program on the US-Mexico border sparked her passion and commitment to utilizing relationship-based methods for transforming conflict. She published her first book in 2013 after completing an MA in International Peace and Conflict Studies at the University of Innsbruck, Austria. She lives in Longmont, Colorado.

Haley Farrar is a restorative practitioner and educator at Victoria University of Wellington and Aspen Restorative Consulting. An attorney and former Fulbright Fellow, she now works with individuals and organizations aspiring to implement restorative practices in their lives and communities. Originally from Richmond, Virginia, Haley currently lives in Wellington, New Zealand.